THE SOVIET SOLDIER

of World War Two

Philippe RIO
PHOTOGRAPHY BY Frédéric COUNE
TRANSLATED FROM THE FRENCH BY Lawrence BROWN

Histoire&Collections

CONTENTS

Note. Even if the publishers chose 'The Soviet soldier' as a title, the man who fought World War Two was actually a Red Army soldier or Frontovik, as the Soviet Army did not appear before 1946. Except where mentioned, all period photographs are from the author's collection.

PREFACE

The preface of a book is usually written by someone involved in its writing or linked with the events that it covers. I will break this rule, but in an indirect way.

In the summer of 2007, whilst on holiday in the Ukraine, I came across a few photos of an artillery officer on a small local market. On the reverse of four of these prints were poems that the lieutenant had written for his mother. This officer's bearing and his moustache suggested that he was from a noble family. The translation of his poems, with their rich vocabulary confirmed that the officer was not just some ordinary Moujik.

These verses also express what we Western Europeans call the "Slav Soul," a mixture of fervour, joy and melancholy.

These poems express the sadness at having left home behind, missing family life, a sense of worry at what returning home would be like and the joy of quickly getting the war over.

I have, therefore, chosen to make these poems part of the preface, along with the photos of this officer, whose name, sadly, remains unknown.

Philippe Rio

The first poem is titled "My dear mother".

"*My dear mother, your son sends his greetings from the front!*
I have not heard from you for some time,
Whilst, behind the bluish mist of the horizon
I walked the paths of my destiny.
I met unhappiness in person
I remember when the cold rains fell
The grey-haired mother welcomed us with a boy
Holding her son tightly against her withered chest.
The pile of ashes still glowed
And the acrid smoke stung our eyes
The wind blowing in abandoned fireplaces

The reverse side of one the photos bearing the poems.

And the rain poured on her silver hair.
In such places we swore where we stood
That the enemy would not know our mercy!
For those who, in tears, called for vengeance
I bear it in my heart like something sacred!
I will overcome all things with rage I believe
In all that fate places in my way
Even if I know that war is not without destruction
I cannot believe in my own death.
When enthusiastically going into combat
I bore your image in my heart
You weep for me, but know that for your son
The enemy will answer for your bitter tears!
Forgive me for only writing these few words
I do not have much time as we leave soon to fight.
I send my greetings to my friends; wait for me along with victory, my dear,
Write to me, your reply will come, I hope."

Poem of 17 December 1944

"*How will you greet me my love?*
If suddenly in front of everyone
I come home safe and sound
From the fight, the fire and smoke?
Covered with the journey's dust
I will not appear to be myself in your eyes.
How will you chase away your worried thoughts?
How will you then come close to me?

Will you walk towards me
Softly uttering my name?
Or like a bird throw yourself into my arms
The heart burning with an ardent flame?

Or will you welcome me like someone unexpected
With surprise in your cold eyes?
Or will you welcome me like a loved friend
Crying tears of joy?

I would like you to welcome me
As before, without fuss and without tears.
That you say nothing of my grey hair
And the wrinkles brought back from the front.

I would like for the difficult moment of our reunion
To be filled with happiness and tenderness.
That joyously we can forget
That the war had separated us."

Poem of 25 December 1944

"*Near the dugout, the cold frost*
Has replaced the summer roses
And, at dawn, in the bluish mist
The broad expanse of ice like fog.

How early autumn comes to us,
How early winter replaces
Storms and fog
By houses of ice

Our years pass in the fighting
Where life is counted in hours,
In the fighting youth goes
And grey hairs appear.

And all that is good and dear in life,
Is covered with a grey dust
And we remember all that is past
Like an unfinished story.

The officer and author of the poems.

In this fighting pass the days and the weeks,
And it is worth giving our lives
So that our children will not go grey
As we go grey in this war.

We are responsible for our happiness
And while remembering the old times
We will proudly show
Our grey hair to our children

Poem of 17 April 1945

"*Do you know mother, I did not think that*
Living in the Donbass of my birth
That we could walk as far
As we have in this war.

We did not have such dreams
Nowhere have I read such bylinas *,
That the road to the house of my birth
Would take me via the German city of Berlin.

You know mother, walking in a foreign country
As a Russian soldier, makes me rightly proud
Because she is now forever free
Our dear great Mother Russia.

I am proud to freeze in a January snowstorm
To have lost a few years in these battles
I am proud to wear the same greatcoat
That the great Stalin wears.

I am also proud as throughout these three years
We might not have survived so many hardships
But only the wrinkles of war have furrowed my brow
As a payment to the great victory.
From the front line of the Great Patriotic War April 1945."

In pencil
"*Greetings to you and my sister.*
I await your letters".

(*) Bylinas are epic narrative poems

Translated by Larissa Guillemet and Victor Suprunyuk

3

On 16 December 1917, Lenin decreed the abolition of the Imperial Army. On 23 February 1918, he announced the creation of the Red Army of Peasants and Workers (Rabochiy Krestyanskaya Krasnaya Armiya-RKKA).

Paradoxically, the very framework of the Red Army was made up of soldiers of the much-hated Tsarist army. Indeed, this decree mentioned the mobilisation of the latter, but also that only the proletariat and Party members would be allowed to join. The former soldiers of the Empire, therefore, continued to serve, strictly watched over by political commissars that guaranteed the revolutionary ideal and devotion to the Communist Party.

During these troubled times, Leon Trotsky, the People's Commissar for War from March 1918 onwards, managed to enforce a return to order and discipline.

Although the Revolution had triumphed in the great cities, the White Armies continued fighting and there was also the conflict against Poland that only ended in 1921. The first campaigns of the Red Army, therefore, took place during a terrible civil war that only ended in a Bolshevik victory in 1923.

With a return to peacetime, the Red Army was at last able to undergo modernisation and, above all, carry out a political cleansing. Distrusted officers were eliminated and replaced with Party leaders. The strength of men serving was reduced and a mixed recruitment system installed (militia and conscription).

Under the leadership of new senior officers (such as Toukhatchevski, chief of staff from 1926 to 1928), new tactical and strategic doctrines were developed.

Top.
One of the numerous official portraits of Vladimir Ilyich Lenin (22 April 1870 – 21 January 1924).

Above.
An official portrait of Ioseb Besarioniq dze Jughashvili, known as *Stalin* ('man of steel'). 18 December 1878 – 5 March 1953.

Furthermore, the growing strength of the Nazi movement in the 1930s worried the Soviet leaders. A second five-year plan was put into place for the Army and it saw its numbers, both in men and materiel increase.

In 1937, the Red Army was confronted with a serious political crisis. The country's leaders feared that the three million military personnel, who lived themselves in fear, would overthrow the regime.

Stalin, head of the CPSU since 1929 and member of the State Committee for Defence, re-established the authority of the political commissars who went on to make sure that the party line was even more strictly adhered to by soldiers and NCOs.

The great purges

On 28 April 1937, a *Pravda* article reminded soldiers that their duty was also "*to be citizens as much as soldiers and to fight the enemy within as well as the foreign one.*"

The implications of this article were immediate: Stalin set about decapitating Red Army leadership. In May 1937, Marshals Toukhatchevski, Blucher and Yegorov were arrested and executed for treason.

However, Stalin's paranoia did not end there, as thirteen out of the fifteen Army generals, 57 lieutenant-generals out of 85, 110 major-generals out of 195 and 220 brigadiers out of 406 were also executed. Only Marshals Budienny and Vorochilov, both unconditional supporters of Stalin, were spared.

This spiral of destruction continued until 1938, when the newly promoted officers were also arrested.

The consequences were dramatic. Despite the young age of the new officers, any sense of initiative disappeared. The lessons at military schools were now nothing more than endless revolutionary tirades!

1 September 1937 saw a new law bringing into effect conscription for all citizens. The numbers in manpower for the

The Osoviakhim parade in Red Square on 1 May 1932.

Red Army increased, but also those of the NKVD (The People's Commissariat for Internal Affairs, the military arm of the Party).

A third five-year plan was based on the development and production of modern weapons.

The Spanish Civil War

During this period, two wars allowed the Soviet command to apply the new doctrines that combined the use of aviation, tanks and artillery.

On the side of the Spanish Republicans, the Soviet officers acted as advisors who, at the same time, tested out the materiel lent by the USSR.

Shortly afterwards, fighting the Japanese in Manchuria allowed them to apply the lessons learnt in the Spanish Civil War. The Battle of Lake Khasan in 1938 and the border incidents of 1939 resulted in Soviet victories and convinced them of their invincibility.

In September 1939, half of Poland was invaded by the Red Army. However, the war in Finland, from November 1939 to March 1940, made the Soviets more wary. Indeed, when using the same tactics as those employed against the Japanese and the Poles, the Soviet command came up against a different type of terrain and adversary.

The first offensives were disastrous and the "steam-roller" tactics did not deliver the hoped-for results.

Here too, the Red Army was able to learn the lessons of a war that cost them 100,000 dead.

Osoviakhim sportsmen parade in Red Square 1 May 1932. Note the rank insignia on the sports clothing.

Below.
Official portrait of Kliment Efremovitch Voroshilov (23 January 1881 – 2 December 1969).

Bottom.
A military ceremony in 1926.

23 August 1939 saw the signing of the German–Soviet Non Aggression Pact. Presented as an economic treaty, it was in fact a political manoeuvre aimed at guaranteeing a certain tranquillity in the Far East. Indeed, Stalin feared being dragged into a war against two enemies - Germany and Japan - and by signing this pact, he protected himself against a Japanese attack as they were allies of Germany.

In 1941, therefore, the Red Army was certain of its superiority. The purges were over, but the commanders still lived in fear of the political commissars and only a small number of officers had any experience in warfare.

As to materiel and logistics, there were still major shortcomings in the fields of signals and medical services. There were plenty of tanks and planes, but the vast majority were obsolete.

The production of weapons remained insufficient, softskin vehicles only numbered 800,000, and a great number of units were still horse-drawn.

One positive aspect however, was the quality of the artillery, which, in that same year, received the first variants of the Katyusha rocket launchers.

In June 1941, the Red Army numbered 177 infantry divisions, 13 cavalry divisions, 230,100 armoured vehicles of various types and 112,000 artillery pieces and mortars. The vast majority of these forces were massed on the western border, as Germany remained the potential enemy.

A CITIZEN UNDER ARMS ★ CHAPTER 1

D uring the Second World War, most Russian soldiers had undergone pre-military training and political indoctrination before 1941.

"The Red Army is invincible"
Pravda editorial– 23 July 1939

From an early age, a form of pre-military training was carried out in schools in cooperation with the Communist Party and the Army. This took the form of the Young Pioneers and the Komsomol (The Communist Union of Youth), then with the paramilitary organisation Osoaviakhim (Society for the defence of the Soviet Union and anti-aircraft defences) created in 1926 and controlled by the Party. This society gave pre-military training in the following fields: marksmanship, flying, parachuting, signals, first aid, horse riding, anti-aircraft and gas defence and mechanics. All young people who successfully completed this training were awarded a qualification badge and a certificate.

Its membership went from 29,500 in 1927 to 1,300,000 in 1941.

Compulsory service

The act of 1 September 1937 brought in conscription for all citizens from the age of 19. As soon as this was set up, there were three age groups constantly serving.

On 1 September 1939, a new bill brought in compulsory military service for all and in 1940, the recruitment age dropped to 17.

Those excluded from military service were all citizens who had been arrested, exiled or deported, as well as foreigners.

Students could obtain a deferment depending on what they studied.

In order to verify his aptitude, the conscript had to undergo a thorough medical examination which resulted in being classified, according to one's aptitude, in one of the five categories

Top.
These Young Pioneers are recognisable by their red ties, held by a brass toggle bearing the emblem of the Pioneers.

Above.
A Young Pioneer's tie toggle.
(Author's photo)

Below.
Osoviakhim members parade in the Donetsk region, 1939.

(A, B, V, G and D) by the conscription commission who decided if the conscript was fit for service, to be postponed, or free from military obligations.

A conscript passed as being fit for service had to carry out five years of military service that was divided into two periods; two years of active service and a three year period in the reserve for privates (three years for NCOs).

Military training comprised of three phases. Upon enlistment and for a day period, the conscripts were assigned to companies under the watch of political commissars.

They were next interviewed in order to check their identity and, if the conscript was a Party member, their reliability. A service number was then attributed.

Then followed a medical and vaccinations. The conscript was then evaluated for assignment to a specialised unit or trade. Uniform and equipment was then issued, along with the Service book.

A second period then followed based on political, military and physical training, then finally, a third period based on unit drill and a more intense political training, making for a total of approximately 45 days. Conscripts were also asked to take part in patriotic debates.

CATEGORIES OF SERVICE APTITUDE

Categories	Remarks
A	Fit for military service.
B	Fit for service with some restrictions, the type of which is indicated by a suffix 1, 2 and so on. Category B excludes service with the parachutists or the Navy.
V	Reduced aptitude for service. The conscript is free from any military obligations, but considered as a reservist. After three years, he is recalled to undergo new examinations.
G	Temporarily unfit/adjourned. The conscript will be recalled after his convalescence.
D	Unfit for service. The conscript is free from military obligations. If his physical condition does not improve, his classification can be examined again.

The distinction between the B and V is extremely subtle, something which allowed some conscripts to attempt avoiding their military service.

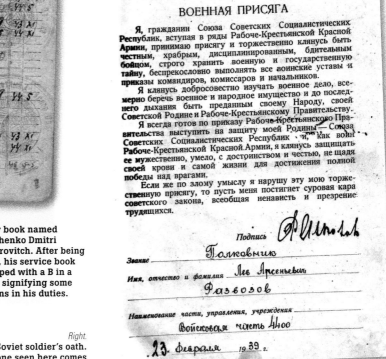

ВОЕННАЯ ПРИСЯГА

Я, гражданин Союза Советских Социалистических Республик, вступая в ряды Рабоче-Крестьянской Красной Армии, принимаю присягу и торжественно клянусь быть честным, храбрым, дисциплинированным, бдительным бойцом, строго хранить военную и государственную тайну, беспрекословно выполнять все воинские уставы и приказы командиров, комиссаров и начальников.

Я клянусь добросовестно изучать военное дело, всемерно беречь военное и народное имущество и до последнего дыхания быть преданным своему Народу, своей Советской Родине и Рабоче-Крестьянскому Правительству.

Я всегда готов по приказу Рабоче-Крестьянского Правительства выступить на защиту моей Родины — Союза Советских Социалистических Республик, и, как воин Рабоче-Крестьянской Красной Армии, я клянусь защищать ее мужественно, умело, с достоинством и честью, не щадя своей крови и самой жизни для достижения полной победы над врагами.

Если же по злому умыслу я нарушу эту мою торжественную присягу, то пусть меня постигнет суровая кара советского закона, всеобщая ненависть и презрение трудящихся.

Подпись

Звание Полковник

Имя, отчество и фамилия Лев Арсеньевич Разоозов

Наименование части, управления, учреждения Войсковая часть 4400

23 февраля 19 39 г.

Tactical training was based more particularly on night-fighting, hand-to-hand and winter combat. The Soviet soldier made do with very little when on campaign; he was naturally tough, skilful and endowed with a talent for resourcefulness. However, he was also characterised by an unfailing obedience.

At the end of basic training, the soldier swore an oath during the course of a political ceremony, whereas the Communist Party considering that from now on, the soldier was indoctrinated and politically reliable.

NCOs were chose by the unit's officers and political commissar. This promotion meant an extra year of service. NCOs also attended classes, or could be promoted directly depending on how they carried out their duties. They were recruited from citizens who had begun their secondary education (six classes). However, there were not enough NCOs in 1941. Indeed, education was compulsory until the end of primary school (4 classes), after which, more often children started working instead of continuing their education.

The Red Army, therefore, had a large number of soldiers, but not enough NCOs, another hindrance was the absence of training schools for them.

When they had completed their service, the citizens were placed in the 1st category reserve with a two-month yearly training period.

Between the ages of 35 and 45, the conscript was placed in the 2nd category reserve with shorter periods of training.

From 45 to 50 years old, the men were placed in the 3rd category reserve.

When war broke out in 1941, the classes serving were those of 1920, 1921 and 1922.

During the "Great Patriotic War", and given the scale of the losses (90% of the men of 1941 were killed, wounded or taken

Red Army book named to Chevtchenko Dmitri Aleksandrovitch. After being wounded, his service book was stamped with a B in a diamond, signifying some restrictions in his duties.

Right.
The Soviet soldier's oath. The one seen here comes from the military files of Major-General Razvozov Lev Arsientievitch, commandant of engineers from 1941 to 1945.

Below, right.
A training camp. The men were housed together in large tents.

Weapons training with the Maxim machine-gun.

THE SOLDIER'S OATH

I, citizen of the Union of Soviet Socialist Republics, joining the ranks of the Red Army of the peasants and workers, take the oath and solemnly pledge to be honest, hard working, disciplined, vigilant, courageous and observe military and state secrets, to observe the constitution of the USSR and Soviet laws, unquestioningly to carry out the requirements of all military regulations and orders of commanders and commissars.

I pledge conscientiously to study military science, to preserve in every way military and public property and to remain devoted till my last breath to my people, my Soviet homeland, and the Soviet government.

I am prepared at all times, on orders from the government, to come out in defence of my homeland, the Union of Soviet Socialist Republics. I pledge to defend it courageously, skilfully, with dignity and honour, without sparing my blood and life in securing complete victory over the enemies.

If I break this solemn vow, may I be severely punished by the Soviet people, universally hated, and despised by the working people.

Рис. 36. Внутренний порядок в казарме

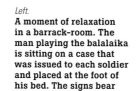

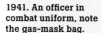

prisoner), basic training was reduced to the bare minimum and men aged between 16 and 50 were automatically drafted.

The directives of the mobilisation plan aimed at each recruitment centre being able to train between 1,200 and 1,500 men in less than 10 days!

As a consequence, units were trained and sent to the front in less than fifteen days. Thanks to the Osoviakhim, a very large majority of recruits had indeed received some military training, but losses were very high once at the front. In 1942, 42% of soldiers mobilised had received less than ten days training, 40% roughly one month and 18% more than one month!

In 1943, a great effort was made to increase the training period for recruits, and the theoretical length of basic training increased from four months to five.

During the course of the summer of 1944, two million recruits from the liberated regions were mobilised, trained and attached to the units of the 1st, 2nd, 3rd and 4th Ukrainian fronts.

Demobilisation

At the end of the war, demobilisation was carried out in stages, the first of these being on 23 June 1945, the second on 7 September 1945 and the last on 23 September of the same year. Service personnel were demobilised according to criteria defined by the presidency of the Supreme Soviet, such as age and profession. Certain trades were given priority, as the Soviet Union badly needed workers and miners to get the country back on its feet. Priority was also given to teachers, veterans who had been wounded at least three times and military personnel mobilised since 1938.

A soldier, who had lost his house or flat, was given a grant depending on the number of years served on the front line. As soon as demobilisation was announced, the soldier was given a transport warrant to travel back to his hometown and a new service book.

Officers

"Any attack against the Soviet Union will come up against the crushing strength of our armed forces."

"If an enemy forces us into war, our Red Army will be the most powerful attacking force ever seen."

An extract from Field service regulations, 1939.

Officers were selected from citizens who had been educated during eight classes (corresponding to the end of the secondary cycle), and aged between 18 and 23 at the oldest, something that ensured political loyalty (members of the Komsomols or the Party).

They also had to take an exam covering the Russian language, mathematics and geography.

In 1941, 70% of officers were of worker or peasant origin. Very few had undergone any military training and their skills were limited. The training period lasted two years in infantry schools and three for technical personnel. During the course of the war, the duration of this training period was reduced to 6 months in some schools.

Upon graduating, the best pupils were promoted *Mladchyi Leitenant* and assigned to infantry or tank units. The others were sent to support units where they had to prove their worth. Throughout their careers, officers had to undergo numerous other periods of military and political training.

Any promotion saw the prolongation of the period of service, two years for a lieutenant and four for a colonel. Promotion for officers was decided upon, along with his superiors, by a political commissar. In order to receive promotion, it was, therefore, a good thing to hold the Party card (in 1943, 75% of those promoted were members). Also, due to the decree of 4 October 1942, the commissars were made regular officers. 1,220 of them went through Army service schools and were commissioned as second lieutenants.

However, during the war, the great majority of subalterns came up from the ranks. Despite being given lessons to

improve their capabilities, they were condemned to remain in the lower ranks.

After the war, officers who had learned their trade at the tough school of the front line became part of the intellectual and moral elite of Soviet society. Their relationship with the other ranks was casual and the term of "comrade" was de rigueur in any conversation.

Women in the Red Army

Contrary to other European nations at the time, the Soviet Union always placed a great importance on women. Although at the beginning of the war, women more often occupied positions in the medical services and signals, they were later found in practically all the arms and services.

Indeed, the appalling losses of 1941 and 1942 led the Soviet government to take drastic measures in order to mobilise the maximum number of men and women.

As the Osoviakhim was open to both sexes, women had already received some military training, allowing them to be attached to anti-aircraft, mortar, tank and aviation units, some of which were exclusively feminine. Female personnel were not assigned to the infantry except for snipers.

Women represented 10% of the armed forces during the Great Patriotic War, making a total of approximately three million women-soldiers.

71 women were made Heroes of the Soviet Union: 27 aviators, 21 partisans, eight snipers, two scouts, a tank crew member and 12 women of the medical services.

Political commissars

The political education of officers and other ranks was carried out by political officers that could be found at every level of command and in all arms.

The corps of political commissars was created in 1918 to keep an eye on the officers of the new Red Army, most of whom, being former officers of the Tsar, were not trusted by the Bolshevik regime that did not yet have any officers of working class origin.

The influence of the commissars, which often had no military qualifications but were totally dedicated to the Communist cause, was disastrous during the conflict with Finland.

Below.
Official photograph of a female Hero of the Soviet Union. Above her medal of Hero of the Soviet Union is the Order of Lenin, the Order of the Red Banner and the Caucasus Defence Medal. She has also been awarded two Orders of the Red Star, an Order of the Patriotic War and below, the Guards insignia.

Below right.
A Red Army female-soldier in 1944. Note the way that she wears the beret, and the large buttons of the greatcoat collar tabs.

However, they also played a fundamental role in resisting the German invasion of 1941, as they knew how to motivate the troops, despite the defection of line officers, but still managed occasionally to make catastrophic decisions.

The commissars had to have good leadership skills and also lead by example, even if it meant sacrificing their own lives. They also had to recruit for the Party worthy soldiers who could serve the cause.

In August 1942, the title of political commissar was abolished to make way for that of "Deputy for Political Matters" so that they would not cause offence to the Western Allies who did care much for this form of politicising.

Beginning in 1943, these deputies at last gained the respect of the ranks. They had by now acquired combat experience and due to the heavy losses suffered by infantry officers, were generally more competent than newly promoted officers. They were listened to by commanders and knew how to defend the men when they warranted it.

Political commissars had to establish that they had been Party members for at least three years, five if the position they wanted was higher up. They were trained in one of the three political schools: Lenin, Engels and Frunze.

The political officer's mission consisted of ensuring the loyalty of Party and Komsomol members in uniform. They

A lecture in an Army service school, 1945.

were tasked with the indoctrination of the ranks, watched over officers and made anti-enemy propaganda. The latter was handed out in all the languages spoken within the Red Army, in the form of pamphlets, slogans and photos that showed German atrocities.

The political officer dispensed daily two hours of political education to the personnel of his unit.

The political officer also organised entertainment for his unit, usually in the form of dances, concerts and reading clubs. He also distributed Party and Army newspapers (*Krasnaya Zveda*, the Red Star), not forgetting the various front line publications. He made sure that the men heard, either by radio or record, Stalin's speeches and the Party news bulletins.

The *Red Star* was a daily newspaper (except for Sundays) aimed at all of the armed forces personnel. It contained general news articles, Headquarters communiqués, the exploits of Soviet troops, as well as promotions and the awards of medals.

The *Army information journal* was printed monthly and had a circulation of 150,000 that were distributed to the commanders of the armed forces. It carried ideological and political articles, as well as news on foreign armies.

The once every two months *Military Bulletin* had a print run of 50,000 and was handed out to commanders of infantry units. It covered the lessons learnt from previous fighting, new tactics and information on new weapons, munitions and materiel.

Each division also had a mobile cinema that showed films considered suitable by the Supreme Soviet, such as propaganda documentaries and patriotic political works like *Alexander Nevski*, *The Rainbow*, *Koutouzov* and *Professor Mamlock*.

Rest and leave

During the entire duration of the war, all leave was cancelled. Only Heroes of the Soviet Union medal were given two months leave upon receiving the award, something that most recipients refused.

Units were given a period of rest behind the front line after spending three months at the sharp end. This period was given over to refitting, both in manpower and materiel, and to military and political training by the political commissars.

Units at rest also dealt with the intake and training of recruits from liberated regions.

"*I was called up on 6 August 1941 and demobbed on 9 January 1947. The only time I ever had any rest throughout the whole war was when I went to hospital for my four wounds.*"

Recollections of Starchiy-Leitenant Riabtchenko Mikaïl Danilovitch. 399th, 206th, 149th and 61st Infantry Divisions.

A rare colour photo showing two political commissars, identified by their sleeve insignia. The commissar on the right is Politruk Kouprianov Ivan Fedorovitch. He was a commissar with the 4th Company, 1149th Regiment of the 353rd Infantry Division from 18 July 1941 until 23 January 1942, the date upon which he was first wounded. When he left hospital, he was given the command of an artillery battery with the 103rd infantry brigade, still as a commissar. On 31 January 1943, he was wounded again. Following his convalescence he was given command of an artillery battery of the 89th Regiment of the 28th Guards Division. He was decorated with the Order of the Red Star in 1945.

Burials

As a rule, the burial of soldiers was accompanied by a ceremony and the Party made the most of the occasion to show its benevolence and gratitude towards those who had died for the Motherland.

At the beginning of the war, however, and due to the disasters that befell the country, a great many dead were at best buried unidentified in mass graves.

If the front was quiet, the dead could be honoured during a straightforward ceremony. The soldiers were wrapped into their greatcoats before being buried; that is unless their uniform was removed to be used again.

If there was a village nearby, its cemetery would be used for the burial of fallen soldiers. They would not receive a religious benediction as the Party encouraged atheism.

Below.
Death certificate for regiment commander Chernetzov Matvej Varlamovitch, born in the Cossack village of Kalitvinskaya. He was killed on 19 November 1943 and buried in the military cemetery of Temryuk town, Krasnodar region. This notice was mailed to his widow Chernetzov Piana Vasiljevna to vouch for her pension rights.

Bottom left.
One of Stalin's orders of the day is read out by a commissar in February 1942.

TABLE OF RATIONS

Foodstuffs	First line troops	Rear area troops
Bread	800 grams	600 grams
Meat	150 grams	75 grams
Fish	80 grams	50 grams
Kacha	140 grams	70 grams
Noodles	30 grams	20 grams
Lard	30 grams	20 grams
Oil	20 centilitres	20 centilitres
Sugar	35 grams	20 grams
Various vegetables	500 grams	400 grams
Salt	30 grams	30 grams
Tea	1 gram	1 gram
Spices	3 grams	3 grams
Tobacco	20 grams	10 grams

Army Fare

With the Soviet soldier being of a rustic nature, he was content with food that could appear as being poor, but it was adapted and evolved depending on the seasons.

During the period of 1941-43, food was a constant problem as the Germans occupied a large part of the Soviet Union and more particularly, the Ukraine, the breadbasket of the USSR.

Shortly after the outbreak of war, the People's Commissariat stipulated, by order No 312 dated 20 September 1941, the amount of rations for soldiers and officers, making a distinction between those who served at the front line and those to the rear.

However, on 1 October, given the way the war was going, rations were once more reduced. From this date onwards, apart from air and naval forces and military hospitals, the armed forces would receive the rations shown in the table above.

A meal was generally made up of *Kacha*, a wheat stew, accompanied by black bread (between 700 and 800 grams) and some pig fat. It was sometimes made with onions, sunflower seeds or sprats (small salted herrings).

Meat disappeared early on during the war and only reappeared with American supplied tins of beef or pork that were part of the lend-lease agreement.

Cigarette paper.

"During the Battle of Stalingrad, we were given 750 grams of bread per day, sometimes with hot water and a handful of flour. With this we were supposed to fight, night and day, in the cold…

We could not wash or shave, nor sleep, but the men understood why."

Recollections of Lieutenant Kravchenko Vladislav Nikolaievitch.

Commander of the 1st punishment platoon of the 57th Army – 199th Infantry Division.

"We ate badly, we were allowed 800 grams of bread a day and occasionally a few frozen potatoes. We walked a lot as we could only move by night and this would last roughly seven hours. This was sometimes pretty tough, especially with a full pack."

Recollections of female Leitenant Sabada Maria Sergeïno-vna, 32nd Guards Division.

Depending on the category to which a soldier belonged, he could receive extra rations such as butter, cream, sugar or jam.

An aviator or a scout received more rations than a basic rifleman. There were eleven various scales of rationing, with the eleventh being reserved for aviators.

On the other hand, it is wrongly believed that vodka was distributed at each meal. The appearance of this alcoholic beverage in the Red Army is down to Marshal Vorochilov in 1942. When troops had to launch an attack, each soldier was given a 150-gram swig by a political commissar. However, as a rule, vodka was drunk by officers only. When water was not available, such as during the Battle of Sebastopol, the troops drank Crimean champagne…

Top.
Extract of the Field regulations showing a field kitchen, here stowed inside a railroad car.

An American lend-lease tin of meat. Inscriptions are both in english and russian.
(Author's photo)

Below.
This rare photo, dated 7 February 1945, shows the burial of an artillery unit commander. This type of photo is very rare due to Russian superstition.

Above.
Regulation red linen tobacco packet.
(Author's photo)

Right.
Machorka tobacco wrapping.

DISCIPLINE

"The commander's order is a law for the subordinate and must be carried out immediately."
Extract from Army regulations

Discipline was maintained by NCOs, officers and, above all, by the unit's political commissar, thanks to constant propaganda. Considered as being proof of loyalty towards the regime, it was not based on fear, but on a sense of duty, a total trust and conscious submission to one's leaders.

The morale of the soldiers was also maintained by a belief in merit and emulation. If a soldier showed exemplary behaviour in combat, as well as at the barracks, he had to be held up as an example to others.

Awards were distributed in a gradual manner and always with the agreement of the political commissar. They were always accompanied by a ceremony that grouped together as many personnel as possible so that they could see the regime's benevolence.

Amongst these awards were:
★ a token of gratitude,
★ a mention in dispatches,
★ gifts (cigarette cases, watches, food),
★ medals or "Excellent soldier" badges.

During the course of the war, new awards were introduced, such as new medals or orders with pay bonuses depending on the reason for the award, removal of disciplinary measures, certificates of gratitude, increase in pensions and invalidity rate.

Punishments

The lazy or negligent soldier was punished, but also re-educated in various ways, such as trial in front of his comrades and self-criticism meetings, the sending of a letter to his factory or kolkhoz, as army units were often patronised by factories, a kolkhoz or a village, a reprimand by a Party cell or a mention in the unit's newspaper.

If the soldier was found guilty of insubordination, assault against a superior, waste or theft, he was then punished with extra tasks, cancellation of leave, arrest (30 days maximum) or sent to a punishment battalion with the possible loss of rank and medals.

Paradoxically, the most extreme punishment was being banished from the Army. Indeed, this was written down in the workbook and meant that the man would never be able to obtain work in a state owned company.

A man deemed to have sullied honour was judged by a "comrades court of honour" made up of soldiers of the same rank. The death sentence was reserved for desertion in wartime.

Punishment units

In the case of absence without leave, the soldier was placed in a punishment battalion for a period of between six and twenty-four months with loss of rank, medals and having this black mark written down in his service book.

Each division also had a disciplinary company led by officers and NCOs chosen for their integrity and political trustworthiness. However, on occasion, punished men of all ranks were given command responsibilities within these companies. In 1944, the disciplinary company became the assault company and was exposed to heavy losses.

The first punishment battalion was formed in August 1942 on the Northeast front and the last assault companies were formed in January 1945 for the Vistula-Oder offensive.

"In 1942, I was given command of the 1st (then 60th) disciplinary company of the 57th Army. This was made up of men who had tried to dodge being mobilised and cowards who had deserted. However, the majority of the men were soldiers who knew their job, but who had suffered nervous breakdowns. The others were common criminals straight out of prisons and who had accepted to "atone for their crimes against the Motherland". These were dangerous men, hostile towards the Soviet regime and who had received no military training whatsoever."

Recollections of Lieutenant Kravchenko Vladislav Nikolaievitch

Often, common criminals were sent immediately to these punishment units where they committed new crimes in the hope of being sent back to prison where they had a better chance of survival…

As for the "special battalions" (*Spetsbat*), these were made up of men considered as being untrustworthy. They included certain ethnic groups such as the Volga Germans, recruits that had lived in occupied regions, and escaped prisoners of war.

In 1940, prisoners repatriated by Finland were sent to camps and were put through exacting interrogation. In 1941, Stalin ordered that all acts of surrender would be punished by death. As soon as a prisoner was liberated, he was handed over to the *Smerch* (Soviet counter-espionage service under the NKVD) where he underwent interrogation. A great majority of these liberated prisoners were sentenced to between ten and twenty years in a camp and some to death.

"I was a Felcher (doctor) with the 142nd Brigade of Marines. I was wounded and taken prisoner during the battle for the defence of Sebastopol. I was sent to a camp in Germany with other female soldiers and I escaped at the beginning of 1945, carrying on the fight, still in the role of doctor until the month of May.
Upon my return, I was interrogated by the NKVD as they wanted to know how I had been captured and the conditions in the POW camp. After this, I was no longer allowed to work as a doctor and I became a midwife."

Recollections of Gaïdoukova Paulina Vassilievna

A

t the beginning of the war the award of medals was rare, but the Soviet command became a little more liberal later.

Although the variety of medals increased rapidly, they were still sparingly awarded. Some were for all ranks, others only for other ranks or just officers. Medals could be awarded to an individual or collectively to units and also posthumously.

If a man or unit was put forward for a medal, this had to be confirmed at every level of command and accompanied by eye witness accounts. For the highest decorations, only the Supreme Soviet was able to confirm their award.

Medals were always noted in the service book. The order, or the medal could be just mentioned, but one very occasionally

AUTHORITIES AWARDING ORDERS OR MEDALS

Supreme Soviet	Marshal's star
	Order of Victory
	Hero of the Soviet Union Star
	Order of Glory 1st Class
	Order of Suvorov 1st and 2nd Class
	Order of Kutuzov 1st and 2nd Class
	Order of Khmelnitsky 1st and 2nd Class
	20th Anniversary of Red Army medal
Defence Commissariat	3rd Class of Suvorov and Kutuzov Orders
Army Group Commander or military council	Order of Lenin
	Order of Khmelnitsky 3rd Class
Army Commander	Order of the Red Banner
Arm of service chief	Order of Glory 2nd and 3rd Class
	Order of the Red Star
	Order of Alexander Nevsky
Brigade or Divisional Commander	Medal for Valour
	Medal for Combat Service

ORDERS AND MEDALS

1. Order of Lenin
2. Hero of the Soviet Union.
3. Order of the Red Banner 1st type
4. Order of the Red Banner 2nd type
5. Order of Alexander Nevsky
6. Order of the Red Star
7. Order of the Great Patriotic War 2nd class
8. Order of the Great Patriotic War 1st class.

Below.
An official photo showing a ceremony for the award of medals at the Kremlin in 1943. The recipients come from practically all arms, including the Navy (below, right). In the centre foreground are the recipients of the most important medals (Red Banner and the Great Patriotic War 1st Type) and, on the sides, those awarded the Order of the Red Star, the Medal for Valour and the Medal for Combat Service.

comes across a note concerning the decision to award the medal or the order's number.

All orders had a number of issue stamped on the reverse. The same applies for the Medal for Valour, Medal for Combat Service, and the Ouchakov and Nakhimov. Each numbered medal or order was accompanied by a named certificate and a booklet that allowed the recipient to obtain a monthly bonus of 25 roubles for the Order of Lenin, 20 for the Order of the Red Banner and so on.

For the medals known as for the "Defence of…" or the "Capture of…", the soldier had to be present during a determined period of time. Thus for instance, many soldiers who were wounded or killed upon arriving in Stalingrad never received this medal, as they had not been on this particular part of the front line for long enough. Medals and orders were worn on the dress and combat uniform.

If the holder of an order happened to die, the decoration was handed back to military authorities. In the case of loss, the holder had to fill in a form explaining how the order was lost and if he required a new one, something for which he will have to pay for. The new decoration was identified by a Cyrillic D stamped on the reverse.

Using a decoration's issue number, one can, in principle, identify the recipient. However, this is not an easy task when the unit's archives were lost or destroyed as was often the case at the beginning of the war.

"I was decorated with the Order of Alexander Nevsky, but I lost it during the dance held in honour of the 3rd victory anniversary. I never asked for an new one as I would have had to have paid for it, and I couldn't afford to."

Recollections of Starchiy-Leitenant Riabtchenko Mickaïl Danilovitch. 399th, 206th, 149th and 61st Infantry Divisions.

ORDER OF PRECEDENCE FOR ORDERS AND MEDALS

★ On the various jackets and tunics, the **medals** are worn on the left hand side and always in the following order:

★ Gold Star Medal of the Hero of the Soviet Union, which is worn above all the other medals and orders.

Next, as close as possible to the front closure buttons, the Order of Lenin, Order of the Red Banner, Order of Glory (3 classes), Medal for Valour, Medal of Uchakov, Medal for Combat Service, Medal of Nakhimov, Partisans medals (2 classes), Medals for the Defence of Leningrad, Moscow, Odessa, Sebastopol, Stalingrad, Kiev, the Caucasus and Polar regions, Medal for Victory over Germany, Medal for the Victory over Japan, medals for the capture of Budapest, Königsberg, Vienna and Berlin, medals for the liberation of Belgrade, Warsaw and Prague, Medal for Work during the Great Patriotic War.

★ **Orders** are worn on the right hand side with the most important being pinned as close as possible to the buttons. For example, the Order of the Red Star will be as far right as possible and the Order of Suvorov 1st Class as close as possible to the buttons.

The order of precedence is as follows: Order of Suvorov 1st Class, Order of Uchakov 1st Class, Order of Kutuzov 1st Class, Order of Nakhimov 1st Class, Order of Khmelnitsky 1st Class; Orders of Suvorov, etc. 2nd Class; Orders of Suvorov, etc. 3rd Class; Order of Alexander Nevsky, Order of the Great Patriotic War 1st Class, Order of the Great Patriotic War 2nd Class, Order of the Red Star.

SOVIET MEDALS AND ORDERS

Orders or medals	Minimum rank required	Established	Number of awards 1941-45
Order of Victory	Army commander	8 Nov. 1943	17
Hero of the Soviet Union Star	Private	16 April 1934	11.635
Order of Lenin	Private	6 April 1930	57.555
Order of Suvorov	Officer	29 July 1942	1st class: 392 2nd class: 2.540 3rd class: 3.449
Order of Kutuzov	Senior Officer	29 July 1942	1st class: 693 2nd class: 3.206 3rd class: 3.258
Order of Khmelnitsky	Officer Private	 10 October 1943	1st class: 347 2nd class: 1.589 3rd class: 3.548
Order of the Red Banner	Private	16 September 1918	297.963
Order of the Great Patriotic war	Private	20 May 1942	1st class: 275.837 2nd class: 733.913

Orders or medals	Minimum rank required	Established	Number of awards 1941-45
Order of Alexander Nevsky	Subaltern	29 July 1942	33.180
Order of the Red Star	Private	6 April 1930	2.860.000
Order of Glory	All ranks	8 November 1943	1st class: 2.562 2nd class: 17.000 3rd class: 200.000
Order of Uchakov	Officer	3 March 1944	
Order of Nakhimov	Officer	3 March 1944	1st class: 82 2nd class: 469
Nahkimov medal			13.000
Uchakov medal	Private	3 March 1944	15.000
Medal for combat service	Private	17 October 1938	2.804.723
Medal for bravery	Private	17 October 1938	1.940.431
Partisans Medal	Private	2 February 1943	1st class: 56.000 2nd class: 71.000

Above.
An extract from the service book of Subkhangulov Khachtuba of the 1070th Artillery Regiment. Page 7 mentions that he was awarded the Medal for Combat Service No 1137190 on 16 July 1944 by order No 047 and a second Medal for Combat Service (No 2289793) on 29 April 1945 by order No 055/4.

ORDERS AND MEDALS

1. Order of Glory 2nd Class
2. Order of Glory 3rd Class.
3. Medal for Valour 1st type
4. Medal for Valour 2nd type
5. Medal of Nakhimov
6. Medal of Uchakov
7. Medal for Combat Service 1st type
8. Medal for Combat Service 2nd type.

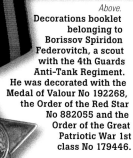

Above.
Decorations booklet belonging to Borissov Spiridon Federovitch, a scout with the 4th Guards Anti-Tank Regiment. He was decorated with the Medal of Valour No 192268, the Order of the Red Star No 882055 and the Order of the Great Patriotic War 1st class No 179446.

Right.
The special booklet for orders and medals.

CAMPAIGN MEDALS

Medals	Minimum rank required	Established	Number of awards 1941-45	Length of service
Defence of Leningrad	Private	22 December 1942	1.470.000	unknown
Defence of Odessa			30.000	10 August - 16 October 1941
Defence of Sebastopol			50.000	5 November 1941 to 4 July 1942
Defence of Stalingrad			760.000	12 July to 19 November 1942
Defence of Moscow		1 May 1944	1.020.000	19 October 1941 to 25 January 1942
Defence of the Caucasus			870.000	1 July 1942 to 30 October 1943
Defence of the Polar regions		5 December 1944	350.000	6 mo. between 22 June 1941 and 20 Sept. 1944
Defence of Kiev		21 June 1961	180.000	
Capture of Budapest		9 June 1945	350.000	20 December 1944 to 13 February 1945
Capture of Königsberg			760.000	23 January to 10 April 1945
Capture of Vienna			270.000	16 March to 13 April 1945
Capture of Berlin			1.100.000	22 April to 2 May 1945
Liberation of Belgrade		9 June 1945	70.000	29 September to 22 October 1944
Liberation of Warsaw			690.000	14-17 January 1945
Liberation of Prague			395.000	3-9 May 1945
Victory over Germany		30 May 1945	14.900.000	
Victory over Japan		9 September 1945	1.800.000	

Bottom.
Documents and medals belonging to Androssiuk Prokop Petrovitch, a corporal telephonist with the 31st Guards Artillery Regiment. He holds the Medal for Valour and the Order of the Red Star. Also shown in this photo are the post-war commemorative medals.

A. Certificate for the award of the Defence of Leningrad Medal.

B. Certificate for the award of the Defence of Stalingrad Medal

C. Certificate for the award of the Capture of Berlin Medal.

15

CAMPAIGN MEDALS

1. Defence of Leningrad
2. Defence of Moscow
3. Defence of Stalingrad
4. Defence of Odessa
5. Defence of Sebastopol
6. Defence of the Caucasus
7. Defence of the Polar Regions
8. Defence of Kiev.

9. Liberation of Belgrade
10. Liberation of Warsaw
11. Liberation of Prague
12. Capture of Königsberg
13. Capture of Budapest
14. Capture of Vienna
15. Capture of Berlin
16. Victory over Germany
17. Victory over Japan.

Commemorative badges

Badge commemorating the Battle of Khasan.

Following the war against Japan, a commemorative badge for the Battle of Lake Khasan was created in 1938.

1939 saw another badge, this time commemorating participation in the Battle of Khalkhin Gol in Manchuria. These two badges were awarded along with a booklet bearing the recipient's photo.

A badge commemorating the fighting on the Finnish Carelia Peninsula was introduced in 1940.

Badge commemorating the Battle of Khalkin Gol.

A drawing of the commemorative badge for Carelia.

Certificates of gratitude

These certificates were awarded to soldiers who had taken part in an important battle or the liberation of a town.

Each certificate was the result of a Supreme Soviet directive and bears a number and date.

There are several patterns, the shape and design differing depending on what materials were available to the propaganda services. Sometimes, these certificates were printed in the liberated towns.

The unit commander decided upon the award of a certificate, which bore his signature and the unit stamp. If a certificate was not available, its award was written down in the service book.

The first certificates were created around February 1943 following the Battle of Stalingrad. With the increasing number of liberated towns and regions, the Supreme Command decided, on 24 July 1943, to attribute numbers to these certificates. Number one was, therefore, officially attributed on 24 July 1943 for the Battle of Kursk and No 373 was in commemoration of the war against Japan.

The actual final certificate, without any order number, was given to all those who took part in the Victory parade in Moscow on 26 June 1945.

Below.
Pages from the service book of Chevtchenko Dmitry Aleksandrovitch of the 1064th Artillery Regiment. The certificates of gratitude are noted down; capture of Lvov in June 1944, capture of the Dombrovsk area on 15 November 1944, the capture of Ratiba on 17 March 1945 and the capture of Berlin on 2 May 1945.

NUMBERING OF CERTIFICATES

Year of award	Numbers
1943	1 to 52 (plus 3 unnumbered certificates)
1944	53 to 218
1945	219 to 373 (plus that of 26 June 1945)

A. The first certificate of gratitude was for the defence of Stalingrad. The crumpled condition of this certificate is due to the fact that the soldiers carried the documents with them.

B. Certificate for the Battle of Stalingrad. The quality of this specimen indicates that it was for officers.

C. Certificate dated 18 January 1945, order No 228, for the capture of Skarnevitch.

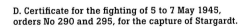

CERTIFICATES OF GRATITUDE

D. Certificate for the fighting of 5 to 7 May 1945, orders No 290 and 295, for the capture of Stargardt.

E. Certificate No 359, dated 2 May 1945 for the capture of Berlin.

F. Certificate commemorating the victory over Germany.

G. Certificate No 372, dated 23 August 1945 to commemorate the fighting against Japan.

17

Guards badge and honorary titles

The title of "Guards" bestowed to a unit dated back to the Revolution and honoured the troops that had distinguished themselves during the Civil War.

On 18 September 1941, Stalin proclaimed that the honorary title of Guards would be given to units that had shown great valour in combat. The first of these were the 100th, 127th, 153rd and 161st Infantry Divisions, which became respectively the 1st, 2nd, 3rd and 4th Guards Divisions on 18 September 1941.

On 21 May 1942, order 167 introduced the Guards badge, which could be awarded on an individual basis or for an entire unit. A soldier could be a member of a Guards unit, but without being a holder of the badge.

The award criteria were similar to those of the excellent soldier badges (see opposite page). The soldier needed to show his dynamism, political zeal and good comradeship throughout his training, or for deeds that would not warrant a medal. The Guards badge was accompanied by a certificate and its award was noted down in the service book.

This award was accompanied by material perks, indeed, Guards units were better equipped when it came to weapons and uniforms. Pay was also higher, as well as supplies, with these units receiving improved rations. On the other hand, the Guards units were always at the forefront and assigned in the most dangerous missions.

In all, 117 infantry, 12 tank, 9 parachute, 17 cavalry, 6 artillery, 6 anti-aircraft and 7 rocket-launcher divisions bore the "Guards" honour title

Formations could also receive an honorary title linked to a battle or the collective award of a medal.

One such example is the 20th Guards Division which illustrated itself during the liberation of Krivoï-Rog, and which, during the course of the war, was awarded the Order of the Red Banner and the Order of Suvorov 2nd Class. Its exact name thus became; 20th Krivorozkaya Guards Division. The Division's stamp mentioned these honorary titles and its flag saw the addition of ribbons corresponding to these orders.

Above.
Colour tinted photograph of an artillery colonel.
He bears on his Mundir tunic two Orders of the Red Star with the Guards badge underneath. He has been awarded the following medals: Combat Service, Defence of Stalingrad, Victory over Germany and the 30th Anniversary of the Red Army.

Above.
A very rare award certificate for the Guards badge.
"For our Soviet Motherland!
This certificate is awarded to Sergeant of the Guards Zalvski Vladimir Gavrilovitch. In virtue of order No 187 of 10 July 1943 of the 1st tank school of the Oulianovsk Guards, decorated with the Order of Lenin and the Order of the Red Star, he received the title of 'Sergeant of the Guards' as well as the badge".
The certificate is attested by the school commander, Lieutenant-General Kachuba, Hero of the Soviet Union. By order of the unit commander, Guards Captain Pronin.

Right.
Pages from the service book of Prokopenko Tikhon Danilovitch, 54th Artillery Regiment, 2nd Guards Infantry Division. The award of the Guards badge is recorded.

1

2

Second World War era Guards badges. The early badges (1) had a slightly rounded shape. The size varied according to the manufacturers (47x35mm, 44x33 mm, 46x35 mm, 45x35 mm, 46x36 mm, 48x36 mm and 47x38 mm.) From 1950 onwards, the red flag featured fringes.

2. The origins of badges on a red cloth backing go back to the Civil War. The fragility of the enamel is obvious with the insignia seen here.
(Author's photo)

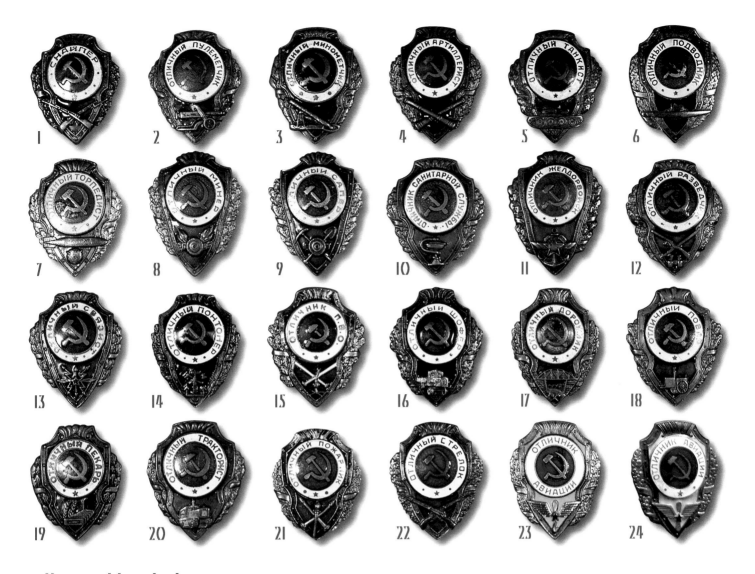

Excellent soldier badges

Badges were created to single out soldiers who proved to be dynamic, skilful and politically motivated. The first "Excellent Soldier" badges appeared in 1921 for the artillery, infantry and cavalry. The badge bore the symbols representing these three arms (rifles, cannons and sabres). These were purely military badges and should not be confused with the Osoviakhim type paramilitary insignia. These badges evolved before taking their final design on 21 May 1942. At the end of the war, there were 24 different types.

Although these badges are frequently seen on period photos, they were awarded according to stringent conditions. Indeed, the soldier had to prove himself both politically and militarily throughout his period of training, then at the front. These badges were only awarded to privates and NCOs and were mentioned in the service book.

The same soldier could be awarded several badges, especially if he was in the artillery. Indeed, a soldier could be named "excellent artillery man," then a "excellent mortar man" as this speciality was a branch of the artillery.

Below.
These tank NCOs wear the same medals and orders. On the left, the Order of Glory, Medal of Valour, Victory over Germany and Liberation of Warsaw. On the right hand side, the Order of the Red Star and Great Patriotic War, Guards insignia, and for the NCO on the left, Excellent Tank Man badge.

Badge	Established
1. Excellent marksman ('Sniper')	21 May 1942
2. Excellent machine gunner	21 May 1942
3. Excellent mortar man	21 May 1942
4. Excellent artilleryman	21 May 1942
5. Excellent tank man	21 May 1942
6. Excellent submariner	21 May 1942
7. Excellent torpedoman	21 May 1942
8. Excellent mine lifter	19 August 1942
9. Excellent sapper	19 August 1942
10. Excellent medical soldier	4 November 1942
11. Excellent railway troops soldier	21 December 1942
12. Excellent scout	10 March 1943
13. Excellent signaller	10 March 1943
14. Excellent pontonier	5 April 1943
15. Excellent anti-aircraft artilleryman	30 April 1943
16. Excellent driver	8 July 1943
17. Excellent pioneer	?
18. Excellent cook	8 July 1943
19. Excellent baker	8 July 1943
20. Excellent machine operator	10 September 1943
21. Excellent fireman	22 November 1944
22. Excellent rifleman	10 June 1947
23 & 24. Excellent aviation soldier (two variants)	1950

MILITARY DOCUMENTS

Army Personal File

A file was compiled for high-ranking officers. It took the form of a blue folder secured by a cloth strap.

The front of the folder bears the rank, surname and first name and to the rear, the photo of the man in question.

It is made up of several parts, the first being the man's civil status, his political background, service records and awards.

The oath is used as a divider and is signed and dated by the soldier.

The second part is the soldier's autobiography where he has to talk about his life without omitting certain details such as his participation in political debates or his membership of certain dissenting movements of the Party.

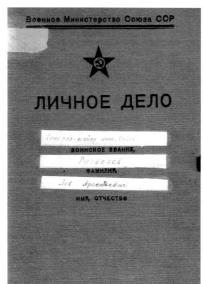

The Army file of Major General Razvozov Lev Arsientievitch, Chief of Engineers from 1941 to 1945.

The third part holds the remarks of political commissars concerning political, military and moral matters.

The second and third parts were updated annually in order to check what the officer had written down and to control his assessment, political and military evolution.

The fourth part held the medical files.

Finally, a fifth part held copies of all the files already held in the other sections just in case any pages disappeared!

Other ranks had a similar file, but it held less information. In the case of a soldier being killed in action, the service book was stapled to the folder, which was then archived.

IDENTITY PAPERS

The other ranks service book

Upon completion of his basic training, the Red Army soldier received a military service book. It measured 7,5 x 11 cm, and had 12 pages. A soldier had to have it on himself at all times.

Right.
Two Red Army soldier service books. Note the differences in the design and the star. The cover is cardboard.

☆ Page 2: Surname, first name, rank and function, recruitment unit, posting, bearer's signature and his photo (the latter is often missing). Service book of Gussarov Trophin Ylisseyevitch, 189st infantry division, 100th medical battalion.

☆ Page 3: Military speciality number, schooling, nationality, year of birth, year and place of recruitment, profession.

☆ Page 4: Address, blood group, vaccinations.
☆ Page 5: Postings.

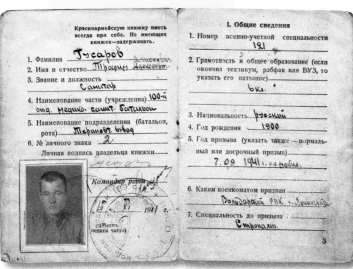

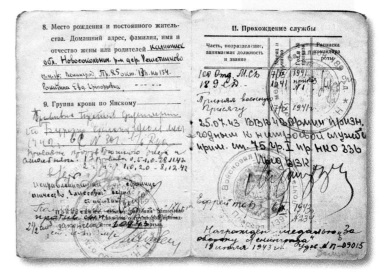

Above.
☆ Page 6
Campaigns, decorations, wounds.

☆ Pages 7 to 10
Uniform and equipment issued along with the date of issue and handing back of any such equipment. Some items issued were written in pen if not on the list. This was more particularly the case with female personnel, tank crew suits, camouflage clothing, special clothing and so on.

☆ Page 7: Schapka, forage cap, cap, greatcoat, wool tunic, cotton tunic, wool trousers, cotton trousers.

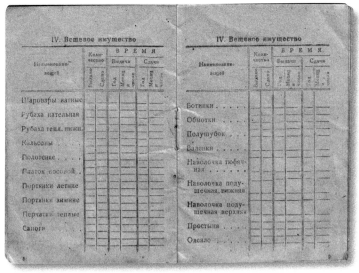

Above.
☆ Page 8: Padded trousers, vest, winter vest, drawers, towel, handkerchiefs, summer socks, winter socks, gloves, and boots.

☆ Page 9: Ankle boots, puttees, short fur coat, felt boots, short coat, mattress cover, pillow cover, sheets, and hood.

Above.
☆ Page 10: Belt, trouser belt, rifle sling, greatcoat strap, pack, special cavalry equipment, grenade pouch, mess tin, water bottle, mess tin cover, water bottle cover.

☆ Page 11: Weapons, technical items, gas mask.

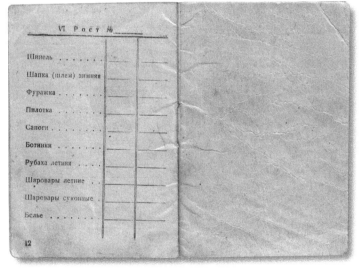

Above.
☆ Page 12: Table of sizes.

Below.
Pages 2 and 3 of the service book made out to Nikolenko Pavel Arsentievitch

OTHER RANKS MILITARY SPECIALITIES

Upon being posted, the soldier was classified in a numbered category corresponding to his military speciality and the arm to which he belonged. This number was found in section 1 on page 2 of the service book.

★ M1 to 5, 5a, 6, 7, 10, 11, 67: rifleman, machine-gunner, loader...
★ 17, 20, 21, 23, 26, 27, 29, 35, 40, 41, 80, 88, 91, 92, 93, 94, 95, 96: technicians, specialists...
★ M 44, 45, 46, 47, 48, 49, 50, 52, 58, 62, 68: signals
★ M 73, 74, 75, 79: Air Force
★ M 109, 113: artillery
★ M 114, 115, 116, 118, 119, 123, 124, 125, 126, 127, 128,131, 132: administration, stableman...
★ M 120, 121: medical services
★ M 133, 133a, 134, 134a: codes associated with stages of enlistment and training whilst awaiting classification in a speciality.

Identity discs

Although its use and issue were not generalised within the Red Army, there was an identity disc (*Litchniy znak*) for other ranks. Made of tin and octagonal in shape, it had a hole at the top for a cord and was marked with the soldier's surname and first name, service number, company number and regiment. It was not issued in peacetime and it would appear that the identity disc was abandoned as early as June 1941, following the high increase in enlistments and the urgency in sending them to the front.

Officers were not issued with an identity tag. They filled in a paper form (17 x 4,5 cm), which, once rolled up, was placed in a waterproof bakelite holder. This holder was carried in one of the tunic breast pockets.

Above.
Part of the regulations introducing the identity disc for other ranks.
It had to be made of metal and be 5 cm in diameter. It bore in clear numbers and letters, the company number, unit name and soldier's service number.

Bakelite holder for the officer's identity document and the other ranks identity disc. The latter bears at the top the words *Litchniy znak* (disc), the company number on the left and at the bottom right the regimental number with, in the centre, the soldier's service number.

Left.
Officer's identity paper, rolled up and placed in the bakelite holder.

Upon demobilisation, the soldier was issued with a reservist service book which bore very precise information on his civil status, social rank, studies, profession, service record and political past. It also re-iterated his obligations as a reservist and mobilisation papers.

Officer's service book

Officers were issued a service book, 7,5 x 11 cm in size and with 17 pages. Inside was the following information: surname, first name, date and place of birth, rank, function and unit, as well as equipment received, successive functions held, promotions, service branch and family details.

Service book belonging to Leitenant Semtchenko Dmitry Antonovitch, of the 911th Artillery Regiment.

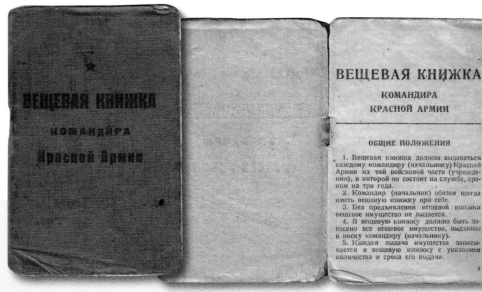

Officer's identity card

These cards of various sizes indicate the civil status, date and place of birth, family status, and always bear the holder's photo. The card notes the man's function and unit, as well as information on the service branch and decorations awarded.

Officer's identity card belonging to Major Pogrebniak Petr Yemelianovitch (card No 159176), of the medical services with casualty clearing station No 2781.

OFFICER'S PAY BOOK

Below.
Pay book belonging to Starshiy Leitenant Liakhovitch Mikhail, issued by the Financial Section of the Defence Commissariat on 2 February 1943.

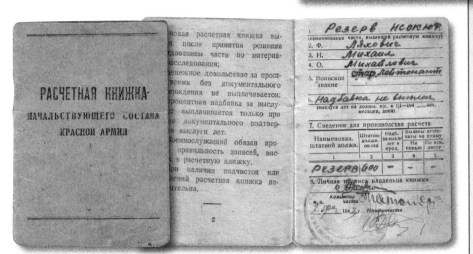

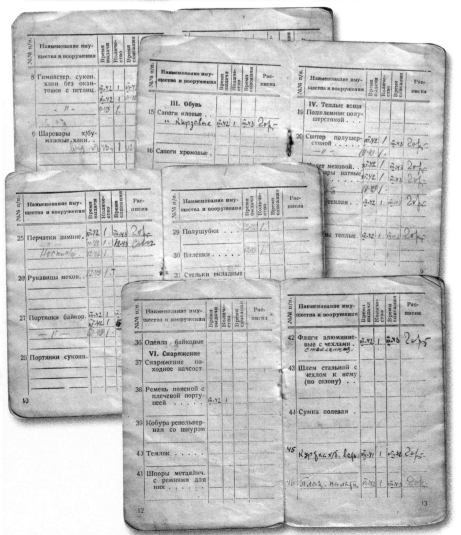

OFFICERS MILITARY SPECIALITIES

The speciality was also identified in the service book by a number, but accompanied by a letter.

Brevet officers
K: Officer with command prerogatives
★ 1, 2, 2a, 4, 5, 9, 9a, 10, 11: infantry...
★ 17, 18: technical services
★ 19, 27, 28, 34, 43, 45, 47, 58: quartermaster, ordnance
★ 66 junior technician
П: political officer
★ 1, 3, 6
Т: technical officer
★ 1, 4, 11, 21, 22, 23
А: administrative officer
★ 1, 4, 5, 6, 25, 55
М: medical officer
★ 1, 50, 53
МБ: veterinary officer
★ 1, 2, 6, 8
Ю: military justice officer
КА: Air Force officers
ТА: Air Force technical officers

Non-brevet officers
МК: Officer with command prerogatives
★ 1, 2, 3, 5, 5a, 6, 7, 10, 21, 30: infantry...
★ 34, 44, 45, 48, 50, 88, 91: technical service
МТ: technical officer
★ 14, 43, 45, 48, 68, 83, 109, 119
ММ: medical officer
★ 121
МБ: veterinary officer
★ 120
МА: medical administration
★ 15, 123, 124, 126, 128

Sometimes a Roman numeral was used to identify a command echelon:

I: platoon
III: company
IV: battalion
V: regiment
VI: brigade or division
VII: army corps
VIII: army
XI: army group or front.

For non-brevet officers, an Arabic numeral was used to identify the command echelon.
1: squad
2: platoon
3: company
4: battalion
5: regiment
6: brigade or division
7: corps
8: army
9: army group or front.

In order to understand more clearly, for instance an officer with the П (P)- 1 – III classification in his service book was a political officer in an infantry company.

Driving licence

This document, 7 X 10 cm in size, comprises of two pages. That of the left bears the holder's photo and the driving licence, as well as the type of vehicle he is authorized to drive. It also bears the stamp of the NKVD unit responsible for the driving test and issuing the licence. It was the same for armoured and other vehicles such as trucks and motorcycles.

Right.
3rd class licence belonging to Pojidayev Andrey Takolevitch, issued on 13 August 1944. It mentions that he may only drive cars.

Below.
Armoured vehicle driving licence issued by the Guards General Leitenant commanding the Tank School, to Guards Sergeant Zalvski Vladimir Gavrilovitch. It is noted that he is a 3rd class mechanic-driver qualified for driving the heavy IS 2 tank. His marks are excellent.

NKVD personnel

NKVD personnel also carried an identity card proving that they belonged to the State security service. The document was renewed annually and changed format in 1943.

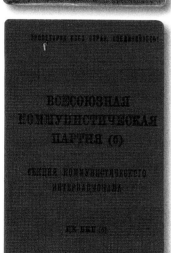

Left.
Communist Party membership booklet issued on 18 November 1943.

Various documents

Of course, if an officer or soldier was a member of the Communist Party or a Komsomol (Communist youth movement), he carried the corresponding identity card. The Party booklet was 7,5 X 10,5 cm in size, and included information on the bearer's identity, photo and card number. The other pages were for subscription payments.

Above and left.
1940 model NKVD card issued on 5 July 1941 to Sergeant Sliptchenko Ivan Grigorevitch, serving in Kirovograd.

Komsomol booklet.

1943 model NKVD card dated 10 March 1945 and issued to Leitenant Joludenko Nikifor Nikitivitch, section No 644.

THE HIGH COMMAND

The State Defence Committee (GOKO)

The State Defence Committee, the GOKO, with Stalin at its head, was made up of members of the government, Molotov (foreign affairs) Vorochilov, Malenkov, Beria, Bulganin, Kaganovitch, Mikoyan and Voznessenski. Created on 30 June 1941, it was dissolved in September 1945.

The Stavka

This was the High Command, created on 23 June 1941 comprising of 12 members (8 officers and 4 commissars) representing each arm and service. In 1945 it had up to 14 members. Amongst these members were: Stalin (Commander in Chief), Kuznetzov (Navy), Novikov (Air Force), Timoshenko (Head of Infantry), Vorochilov (partisans), Voronov (artillery), Fedorenko (armour), Budienny (cavalry) and Vorobev (technical services).

Below.
Marshal Budyonny, commander of cavalry, and Marshal Voroshilov, commander of partisans.

The boards

All work, projects and plans concerning weapons and services were placed under the responsibility of these boards, of which there were ten: aviation, armaments, artillery, ammunition, armour, signals, chemical units, internal affairs (NKVD), transport, quartermaster.

The military regions

Due to the size of the country, the Soviet Union was divided up into five military regions (Leningrad, Riga, Minsk, Kiev and Odessa), commanded by a general.
The naval forces were divided up into fleets: North, Black Sea and Pacific, but also flotillas: Dnieper, Amur, Danube and Sungari.

Districts and commissariats

Next, the military regions were divided into districts, of which there were 31 with HQ usually situated in the largest town.
The district's military commissariat (RVK) was responsible for conscription, mobilisation and the control of military personnel who had completed their military service.

Above.
Marshal Stalin in 1945.

BUDYONNY   VOROSHILOV

Below.
Marshals Timoshenko (infantry), Voronov (artillery) and Rotmistrov (armoured troops).

TIMOSHENKO   VORONOV   ROTMISTROV

Below.
Marshals Golovanov (aviation), Peresypkin (signals), and Fedorenko (armoured troops).

GOLOVANOV   PERESYPKIN   FEDORENKO

MILITARY DISTRICTS, 1941-45

Districts	HQ	Geographic region	Divisions levied, 1941-45
White sea	Kemi	Petsamo, Murmansk, Carelia, Arkhangel	13
Leningrad	Leningrad	Leningrad, Vologoda	16
Baltic	Riga	Estonia & Latvia	
Lithuania		Lithuania	
Minsk	Minsk	Belarus, Vitebsk, Minsk, Moghilev, Gomel	
Lvov	Lvov	Lvov	
Carpathians	(?)	Moldavia	
Kiev	Kiev	Jitomir, Kiev, Chernigov, Kamenents, Vinnitsa	13
Odessa	Odessa	Odessa, Kirovograd	12
Moscow	Moscow	Kalinin, Yaroslav, Smolensk, Moscow, Tula, Ryazan	137
Gorki	Gorki	Ivanovo, Gorki	
Voronej	Voronej	Voronej, Tambov	
Orel	Orel	Orel, Kursk	
Kharkov	Kharkov	Dniepropetrosvk, Poltava, Kharkov, Stalino, Vorochilovgrad	18
Tauric	Simferopol	Nicolayev, Zaporozhiye	
Kazan	Kazan	Kirov	
Volga	Kuibyshev	Penza, Kuibyshev, Saratov	34
Steppe	Stalingrad	Stalingrad, Kalmyk	
Don	Rostov	Rostov	
Kuban	Krasnodar	Krasnodar	
Stavropol	Vorochilov	Ossetia, Tchechnia, Armenia,	47
Tiflis	Tiflis	South Ossetia, Georgia, Inguchetia, Abkhazia	
Baku	Baku	Azerbaïdjan, Nagorno Karabakh	
Ural	Sverdlovsk	Komipermyak, Perm, Sverdlosk	33
South Ural	Chakalov	Bashkir, Chakalov, Kazakstan	
Central Asia		North Kazakstan, Kustanay, Pavlodar	19
Turkestan	Tachkent	Kirghizistan, Uzbekistan, Turkmenistan	
West Siberia	Novossibirsk	Omsk, Yamalo, Altai Krai	16
East Siberia	Irkutsk	Krasnoïarsk, Irkutsk, Mongolia	16
Trans-Baïkal	Tchita	Tchita, Buryat, Yakutsk	9
Eastern	Khabarovsk	Kamchatka, Amur, Koryak	23

VASILEVSKY   SHAPOSHNIKOV   ZHUKOV

Below.
Marshals Koniev, commander of the 2nd Ukrainian Front, Govorov (Leningrad Front), and Rokossovsky (1st Belorussian Front).

KONEV   GOVOROV   ROKOSSOVSKY

VOROBYEV   YAKOVLEV   NOVIKOV

Left.
Marshals Vassilevsky, commander of the 3rd Belorussian Front, Shaposhnikov (infantry commander), and Zhukov.

Below left.
Marshal Vorobiev (technical troops), Yakovlev (artillery) and Novikov (air force).

Bottom.
Soviet officers study a map. The reverse of the photo bears the caption: *"To my mother, from her son Yacha. I am with my brothers in arms in the town of Stariy Oskol."*

The Eastern Front

The Eastern Front was a theatre of operations covering a huge area. In order to ease the command structure, in 1941 the Soviets divided it up into fronts. The latter was the equivalent of an army group and comprised, on average, of one million men covering a frontage of approximately 250 km.

A front was made of four to five infantry armies, one to two armoured armies, one to two air armies, four artillery divisions, five anti-aircraft divisions, five rocket-launcher brigades, two mortar brigades, four heavy artillery brigades, five anti-tank brigades, two armoured corps and one to two mechanised infantry corps.

The army

As with other armies, its composition evolved depending on the fighting and needs. Its frontage was approximately 75 km. The shock army was an infantry army reinforced with armoured units.

The army corps

There were two types of army corps. The mobile army corps and the operational corps. The first was mainly made of artillery and infantry, the latter mostly fielded cavalry, mechanised troops and tanks.

FRONTS PER YEAR

Fronts are indicated from North to South, right column is the name of the front overall commander.

1941

Volkhov Front	Meretskov
Northwestern Front	Kurochkin
Kalinin Front	Konev
Western Front	Joukov
Southwestern Front	Timochenko
Southern Front	Cherevichenko

1942

Volkhov Front	Meretskov
Northwestern front	Kurochkin
Kalinin Front	Konev
Western Front	Joukov
Briansk Front	Cherevichenko
Voronej Front	Golikov
Southwestern Front	Vatutin
Don Front	Rokossovski
Stalingrad Front	Yeremenko
Caucasus Front	Tiulenev

1943 (First semester)

Volkhov Front	Meretskov
Northwestern front	Popov
Kalinin Front	Yeremenko
Western Front	Sokolovski
Belarus Front	Rokossovski
Steppe Front	Konev
Southwestern Front	Malinovski
Southern Front	Tolbukhin

1943 (Second semester)

Volkhov Front	Meretskov
2d Baltic Front	Popov
1st Baltic Front	Bagramyan
Western Front	Sokolovski
Belarus Front	Rokossovski
1st Ukrainian Front	Vatutin
2d Ukrainian Front	Konev
3rd Ukrainian Front	Malinovski
4th Ukrainian Front	Tolbukhin
Caucasus Front	Petrov

1944

Leningrad Front	Govorov
3d Baltic Front	Masslenikov
2d Baltic Front	Yeremenko
1st Baltic Front	Bagramyan
2d Belarus Front	Zakharov
1st Belarus Front	Rokossovski
1st Ukrainian Front	Konev
4th Ukrainian Front	Petrova
2d Ukrainian Front	Malinovski
3rd Ukrainian Front	Tolbukhin

1945

Leningrad Front	Govorov
3d Baltic Front	Masslenikov
2d Baltic Front	Yeremenko
1st Baltic Front	Bagramyan
3d Belarus Front	Malinovski
1st Belarus Front	Rokossovski
1st Ukrainian Frontn	Konev
4th Ukrainian Front	Petrov
2d Ukrainian Front	Malinovski
3rd Ukrainian Front	Tolbukhin

THE COMBAT ARMS
INFANTRY

I N 1941, an infantry division was made up of 18,841 men. Its transport was mostly horse drawn, as it had 6,208 horses compared to 817 trucks and tractors and 28 armoured cars.

Between 22 June and 31 December 1941, the Red Army lost 4,473,820 men. Because of these disastrous losses, the State Defence Committee decided to reduce the division's manpower to 10,790 men. This reorganisation was obtained

to the detriment of artillery regiments and technical troops. Thanks to these measures, fifty-five new divisions were formed between June and July 1941, with a further one hundred and seventeen divisions between August and December. The total number of divisions is as follows: 170 on 22 June 1941, 250 on 1 October, 270 on 1 December and 326 on 1 January 1942.

Between June 1941 and July 1942, the Soviets lost a further 140 divisions, officially destroyed during the great encirclement battles such as Bialystok-Minsk (10 divisions), then Smolensk (12 divisions), Uman (15 divisions), Kiev (34 divisions), Vyazma-Bryansk (36 divisions), Kharkov (18 divisions), Kertch-Crimea (8 divisions) and Sebastopol (7 divisions). Furthermore, 41 divisions were lost on other parts of the Front.

It was only the rapid mobilisation of men and women which allowed to make good these losses and create new formations.

In 1942 divisional strength increased to 12,725 men, falling to 10,400 in July and 9,430 men in December. This was due to an increasingly large front. In December 1944, divisional strength rose to 11,700 men, remaining at this level until 1945.

Top.
Platoon NCOs before going into action in the spring of 1942. Note that one of the soldiers wears a helmet, and the presence of a woman, the latter is in all likelihood one of the unit's medical personnel.

Above.
A group of Soviet soldiers captured by the German Army in the autumn of 1941.

This evolution is comparable to the numbers of vehicles, as motorised vehicles fell to 124 in 1943, rising to 445 in 1945.

According to numbers and their mission, divisions were classed in the following way:
★ Category A: assault division, strength 12, 000 men
★ Category B: normal division, strength 9, 000 men
★ Category V: defence division, strength 6, 000 men.

Mountain troops

In 1941, there were six mountain divisions in the Kiev Military District (44, 58, 60, 72, 96 and 192nd), one in Northern Caucasus (28th), seven in the South Caucasus (9, 20, 47, 63, 76, 77 and 138th), three in Central Asia (68, 83 and 194th), one in the Far East (101st) and one (the 30th) with the 9th Army.

Apart from the 28th Division, which fought with distinction, the others were rarely used. The High Command, therefore, decided to convert them into standard infantry divisions.

The mountain division had a strength of 14,163 men.

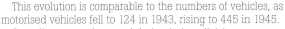

STRENGTH AND ARMAMENT OF THE INFANTRY DIVISION, 1941-44				
	1941	**1942**	**1943**	**1944**
Strength	10.790	9.373	9.534	9.425
Rifles	8.431	6.474	6.274	6.330
SMG	171	894	1.460	2.110
LMG	162	490	490	494
Heavy MG	108	110	110	111
Anti-tank rifles	182	132	132	12
50-mm mortars	54	54	56	0
82-mm mortars	18	85	84	83
120-mm mortars	6	18	18	21
Anti-tank guns	18	48	48	48
76-mm gun	12	12	12	12
122-mm gun	8	20	20	24
Light cars	--	5	5	5
Trucks	200	312	130	120
Tractors	5	15	15	15
Motorcycles	4	4	4	4
Railway cars [1]	673	728	446	395
Carriages [2]	124	342	34	238
Field kitchens	96	82	63	39
Horses	2.468	2.188	1.700	1.732
Radios		61	57	59

1. Number of cars required for train movement of complete division.
2. Horse-drawn division.

Left.
These soldiers perched on a truck are not travelling in comfort, but have avoided a long march. The armament is the Mosin 44 carbine, recognisable by its integral bayonet. Note also the young soldier at the rear and the American Studebaker truck.

★ Baltic Fleet: a total number of 125,000 men, forming 11 brigades that saw action mostly on the Leningrad Front.
★ Black Sea Fleet: a total of 57,197 men, forming 12 brigades that fought in the defence of Odessa and Sebastopol in Crimea, 1943-1944.
★ Northern Fleet: a total of 39,281 men. These units were used in the defence of Murmansk and the coastline.
★ Pacific Fleet: 149,264 men. In 1945, the Naval Infantry captured the Japanese Sakhalin and Kuril islands.

"When I had completed my basic training, I was assigned to the 55th Guards Infantry Division; I was just a private, but my military pay book was marked 'Naval Infantry.' We had the standard uniform, but our tunic had black shoulder boards with the letters BF (Baltic Fleet)."

Recollections of Podernya Paviel Kornieyevitch. 55th Guards Infantry Division

Below.
A Naval Infantry sergeant, once again recognisable by his belt buckle. He wears the type 1935/43 Army blouse with Naval Infantry shoulder boards (black with red piping). Also note the Guards Badge.

A Naval Infantry soldier, recognisable by his navy belt buckle and, on his chest, the Order of Nakhimov (in the centre and which should be closer to the buttonhole) which was only awarded to naval personnel.

Ski troops

During the war against Finland, entire infantry and armoured units had been destroyed by Finnish skiers dashing from the dense woods, then disappearing just as quickly after having inflicted heavy losses.

The first Soviet ski unit was formed in 1940 in Carelia, from elements of the 24th Cavalry Division. In 1941, the ski detachments were in Archangel, Siberia and in the Urals. They were used as instructors for future divisional ski scouts.

Naval troops

In 1941, a large part of the Soviet Fleet was in docks as the armament plans had concentrated on tanks and aircraft. War did not improve the situation, as the tons of steel required for shipbuilding were used instead for the production of badly needed tanks.

The Soviet Navy, therefore, had a large number of personnel, but very few ships. The sailors were thus used to guard naval bases and for coastal watch. However, some naval units fought with distinction around Leningrad and Tallinn in 1941. The High Command then decided to use these troops as naval infantry.

Nicknamed the "Black Death" by the Germans, the Naval Infantry were tenacious fighting men, despite being lightly armed. There were 42 naval infantry brigades, distributed in the following way:

PARACHUTISTS

Pioneers in this field, the Soviets established airborne units as early as 1929.

Indeed, in Central Asia, the *Basmachi*, or anti-communist insurgents, carried out a relentless guerrilla war. A group of fifteen men was parachuted in and used in an operation against the insurgents. This raid was a success and the Red Army immediately thought of large scale operations. The first parachute (*Desantniki*) unit was created in the Leningrad District in 1931 and comprised an infantry company, a sapper platoon and a signals platoon, totalling 164 men. It should be noted that this unit was attached to the Air Force.

Once more, the Osoviakhim paramilitary organisation played an important role, as it trained the future parachutists and glider pilots in its 20,000 schools.

The parachute arm grew in strength on 11 December 1932 with the creation of twenty-nine 800-men battalions.

In 1935, the parachute arm took part in its first manoeuvres. Watched by the high command, a battalion of five-hundred men was on the ground in less than three minutes! In 1936, 5,700 men were dropped in ten minutes during joint manoeuvres with the 84th Infantry Division at Gorky.

In 1938, there were six parachute brigades, each with a strength of 3,000 men.

In 1939, the 221st and 212th Brigades fought against the Japanese at Khalkin Gol. Then, in June 1940, the 201st, 204th and 214th Brigades took part in the occupation of Bessarabia and carried out their first drops.

During the German invasion, the parachutists were used as regular infantry and suffered heavy losses due to their light armament. It should be mentioned that the Soviet Air Force had been practically wiped out and that there were hardly any transport aircraft to carry the parachutists for airdrops. However, during the winter of 1941-1942, men were dropped into the Viazma sector in order to destroy the German forces encircled in this pocket. This operation was a partial failure as the Germans managed to break out.

In 1942, the Soviet command decided to convert the parachute troops into Guards infantry units. Within less than fifteen days they were sent to Stalingrad where they distinguished themselves.

In September 1943, parachutists were at last dropped in order to assist ground troops in their crossing of the Dnieper River. One again, a lack of coordination resulted in failure, as the troops were scattered over a large area of 900 square kilometres instead of a 100! The survivors joined partisan units.

Between 18 and 27 August 1945, parachutists were in action against the Japanese in Manchuria and during this fighting, they occupied several towns and captured the last Chinese emperor.

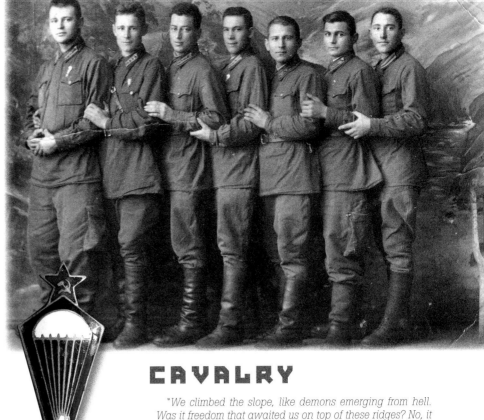

Parachutist badge,
1936-1941 Pattern.

Top right.
This photo of a group of parachutists bears the inscription: "Vassia Roudenko 20 January 1942. Lest we forget the parachutists, joyful lads, full of life, especially Vassia!"

Left.
Three parachutist lieutenants. The parachute badge is worn above the M.35 tunic's left pocket. The parachutists being an integral part of the Air Force, they wear its insignia on the collar tabs.

Below.
Cavalry on the march west of Rostov-on-Don in March 1943.

CAVALRY

"We climbed the slope, like demons emerging from hell. Was it freedom that awaited us on top of these ridges? No, it was the Red Army Cossacks!

Suddenly, they charged down the slope, screaming, brandishing their sabres. They charged at us in the same centuries old way, the Cossacks, galloping straight ahead and without pity."

From the memoirs of Paul Terlin, A Belgian volunteer with the German army.

Although other countries had reduced their cavalry units, the USSR fielded 13 such divisions in 1941. With a strength of 60,560 men, they were used in the war against Poland in 1940. However, in 1941, the cavalrymen were powerless against German tanks and suffered heavy losses. The High Command created twenty new light cavalry divisions (30,500x men) in less than three weeks.

In the republics, ethnic "horsemen", hostile to the Party, were mobilised by being called upon to defend the Motherland rather than communist values. This allowed for the creation of 37 divisions of Central Asian, Ural and Caucasian origin. They were used as cannon fodder, often in an infantry role.

On 1 May 1943, the USSR had 26 cavalry divisions with a total strength of 238,968 men and 226,816 horses. These numbers decreased, as some of these formations were motorised. However, the real cavalry maintained its importance until the last months of the war. The vast front and huge territories and forests allowed the cavalry to be efficiently deployed. During the muddy Rasputitza period, they were the only units still capable of manoeuvring.

The Cavalry distinguished itself during the fighting to reduce the Korsun Pocket in 1944. The German forces were

A souvenir photo of three cavalrymen, recognisable by their Shashka sabres. The collar patches, as well as the Budenovka headwear are in cavalry colours of dark blue with black piping.

disorganised and lacked air support, so the Cavalry took care of the last pockets of resistance. The strong psychological impact that these heavy charges had on the Germans should not be forgotten. These cavalry divisions were able to travel hundreds of kilometres in a few days and suddenly appear behind the front lines.

ARTILLERY

In June 1941, the Red Army artillery could field 112,000 guns and mortars, a much higher number than any other European army. Many of these guns had been designed with German help during the inter-war period. The artillery units were mostly equipped with 76 mm and 122 mm guns.

However, between June and December 1941, the Red Army lost 40,600 guns of all calibres and 60,000 mortars. In record time, artillerymen were trained and equipped with more modern materiel (radios, range tables, etc.). The ordnance was modernised with the onus being placed on anti-tank guns and light guns.

Production of 203-mm and 152-mm guns was slowed down in order to manufacture 57-mm, 76-mm, and 122-mm guns.

New production methods led to a reduction of the manufacturing process of 76-mm guns (1,029 hours in 1942, 475 in 1944).

Anti-aircraft artillery comprised of a full range of double or quadruple machine-guns mounts, as well as several guns.

Anti-tank artillery

As a defence against the Panzers, the Soviets sought an early development of anti-tank guns. Well before war broke out, anti-tank brigades had been created, armed with 76-mm, 85-mm and 107-mm guns. However, they were mostly horse-drawn and could not match the rapidity of the German troops during Operation Barbarossa. In 1942, 122 anti-tank artillery regiments were formed, to which were added sappers specialised in laying mines, but the new German tanks meant that the Soviets had to constantly upgrade their guns and ammunition.

Stalin's organs

The famous *Katyusha*, or "Stalin's Organs" rocket-launchers were also operated by artillerymen. Their code name was "Guards Mortars" as the Soviets cloaked these weapons in great secrecy.

The first rockets were fired from aircraft against the Japanese at Khalkin Gol in 1939. Truck-borne launchers were next designed, firing their first salvos in July 1941 at Orsha. The new weapon was a success; in a short space of time, a sector could be saturated with rockets which had a strong demoralising

Below.
The M.42 anti-tank gun.

effect on enemy troops. The first vehicle models were the BM8, a modified ZIS-6 truck and which could launch a salvo of 36 rockets, and the BM8-24 which fired a salvo of 24 rockets. T-40 and T-60 tanks were also adapted to carry rocket launchers, but in the end, there were 18 automobile launchers and sixty different chassis.

The tactical doctrine of the artillery changed during the course of the war, with the Red Army undertaking a sustained barrage of enemy lines before each offensive. Every attack, be it by infantry or tanks, was preceded by a heavy bombardment.

During the Battle of Stalingrad, there were 330 pieces of various calibres per square kilometre, and for the capture of

MORTARS

	calibre	weight	max. range	shell weight
M.38	50	14	800	0.900
M.40 & M.41	50	12	800	0.900
M.37	82	61	3.100	3.400
M.41	82	50	3.100	3.400
M.41-42	82	44.5	3.500	3.350
M.38 (mountain)	107	170	6.300	8.00
M.38	120	256	5.700	16.400
M.38-43	120	280	5.700	16.400

ARTILLERY PIECES

	calibre	weight action/limbered	max. range	Shell wt. HE/AP
Infantry guns				
M.27 Howitzer	76.2	800/1.600	8.570	6.5
M.43 Howitzer	76.2	600	4.200	6.5
Mountain guns				
M.38 Gun	76.2	785	10.100	6.2
Field guns				
M.36 Gun	76.2	1.620/2.820	13.580	6.4
M.39 Gun	76.2	1.480/2.500	13.300	6.2
ZIS M.42 Gun	76.2	1.120/2.500	12.900	6.2
M.44 Gun	100	3.650/4.300	21.000	15.6
M.10-30 Gun	106.8	2.380/2.580	16.100	16.8
M.40 Gun	107	4.000/4.300	18.000	18.8
Howitzer M.10-30	122	1.470/2.380	8.900	21.7
M.31-37 Gun	122	7.100/7.930	20.400	25.0
Howitzer M.38	122	2.260/2.900	11.800	21.7
M.10-34 Gun	152	7.100	16.000	40.0
M.35 Gun	152	17.200/18.260	27.000	49.0 [1]
M.37 Howitzer	152	7.130/7.930	17.200	43.6
M.38 Howitzer	152	4.150/4.550	12.400	40
M.43 Howitzer	152	3.600/3.640	12.400	40
Anti-tank guns				
M.37 Gun	45	510	4.400	1.4/2.2
M.42 Gun	45	570	4.400	1.4/2.2
M.43 Gun	57	1.150	5.200	3.1/4.2
ZIS M.42 Gun	76.2	1.120	12.900	6.2 [2]
M.45 Gun	85		15.500	9.0
M.44 Gun	100	3.650	21.000	15.6

Anti-aircraft artillery

	calibre	rate	range
Degtyarov MG	7.62	550	1 000
Degtyarov M.38 Dchk MG	12.7	575	1 500
Degtyarov M.40 MG	12.7	575	2 000
M.39 Gun	37	180	4 000 [3]
M.31 Gun	76.2	20	9 300 [3]
M.38 Gun	76.2	20	9 500 [3]
M.39 Gun	85	20	10 500 [3]
M.42 Gun	85	20	11 000 [3]

Katiusha rocket launcher

	calibre	N. of rounds	range	rocket weight
M.8	82	32 à 48	5.300	6.860 [4]
	105		6.000	
M.8 (AA type)	80	4		
M.13	130		6.000	25.000
	132	16	8.470	42.600 [5]
	135		8.870	42.600
	140		4.980	42.600
M.30	300	12	2.500	80.800
	400		2.800	76.500

1. Tracked mount
2. Field gun
3. Heavy AA
4. Rocket measures 70 cms + fins
5. Truck-mounted.

Above.
The M.43 anti-tank gun.

Berlin, this number increased to 620 guns per square kilometre. A total of 22,000 tons of shells were fired into the city. All throughout the war, the Soviet artillery was of excellent quality. Straightforward and robust, it went from 15% to 50% of the strength and means of the Army.

Below.
Katiusha 82-mm rocket launcher, mounted on an American lend-lease Studebaker truck.

Bottom.
Soviet artillerymen in the autumn of 1941. The gun is the model 27 76,2-mm infantry howitzer.

TANKS

The first nation to experiment in the massed use of tanks, the Soviet Union was a pioneer in this field.

In 1930, tank regiments were formed, as well as motorised infantry regiments. The tactical doctrine for tanks was to use them for breakthroughs, with aviation support. Indeed, the fifth five-year Plan was almost solely aimed at the development and mass production of new tanks.

In 1936, the USSR supplied 362 tanks and 120 armoured cars to the Spanish Republicans. An armoured division was formed under the command of General Pavlov. Upon his return to the Soviet Union, Pavlov recommended a new tank doctrine. Indeed, contrary to the Germans, the Soviets were disappointed in the tanks, which were too vulnerable to mines and other anti-tank weapons. They came to the conclusion that the tanks could not take part in offensive action.

During the fighting at Khalkin Gol in 1939 against the Japanese, Zhukov nevertheless managed to convince the General Staff to use tanks in the attack. However, in Finland, the terrain did not lend itself to the use of armour and losses were huge (3,500 tanks). Serious deficiencies also became apparent: lack of on-board radios, fuel and ammunition supply problems.

Measures were taken to correct these deficiencies, but the brutal German attack reduced all of these efforts to nothing.

In 1941, many Soviet tanks were obsolete and the new models not yet under mass production. On 1 June 1941, 263 KV-1, 70 KV-2 and 1,085 T-34 tanks rolled off the assembly lines. Given the number of armoured units, 3,483 KV and 12,810 T-34 tanks were missing.

Despite the experiences in Spain and Finland, the tanks were very badly handled. There was no coordination with the other units, with each division using its tanks at any given time and without infantry support. The number of tanks lost in 1941 was 20,500! The defence of Moscow in the winter of 1941 cost an extra 1,386 tanks.

SOVIET TANKS PRODUCTION TABLE

Type	1941	1942	1943	1944	1945	TOTAL
Heavy tanks						
KV-1	1.121	1.753	0	0	0	2.874
KV-2	232	0	0	0	0	232
KV-1 S	0	780	452	0	0	1.232
KV-85	0	0	130	0	0	130
IS-II	0	0	102	2.252	1.500	3.854
Medium tanks						
T-34/76	3.014	12.553	15.529	2.995	0	34.091
T-34/85	0	0	283	11.778	.230	23.661
Light tanks						
T-44	0	0	0	0	200	200
T-40	41	181	0	0	0	222
T-50	48	15	0	0	0	63
T-60	1 818	4.474	0	0	0	6.292
T-70	0	4.883	3.343	0	0	8.226
T-80	0	0	120	0	0	120
Assault guns						
SU-76	0	26	1.928	7.155	3.562	12.671
SU-85	0	0	750	1.300	0	2.050
SU-100	0	0	0	500	1 175	1.675
SU-122	0	25	630	493	0	1.148
SU-152	0	0	704	0	0	704
ISU-122	0	0	0	1.600	800	2.400
ISU-152	0	0	35	900	400	1.335

Top left.
This Starshiy Serzhant of an armoured unit has attached a red star to the top of his padded tank helmet.

KV-1 heavy tank.

Light tanks T-50, T-60 and T-70 (M).

The lesson was hard learnt and the Soviets changed tactics. Starting at the end of 1942, the tanks attacked in groups and in a more flexible manner. They systematically benefited from infantry support. The tanks were equipped with radios, extra fuel tanks, and the engines and chassis were standardised.

Crews were also better trained. Indeed, at the beginning, the training of tank crews took a considerable amount of time and there was a lack of crews. NCOs and officers were often transferred to the infantry and artillery. Many tank crew only had one of two hours of driving on the new tanks! From 1944 onwards, the crews had, on average, fourteen hours of driving before graduating and being sent to the Front.

Medium tanks T-34/76 and T34/85

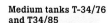

THE SERVICES
SIGNALS

Right.
**The UNA-J
field telephone.**

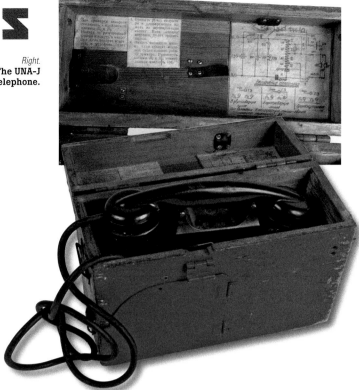

In 1941, the Soviet signals units had been neglected for other arms and services. Although great strides had been made in the field of power amplifiers and frequencies, production had not kept up. Units were still equipped with fixed communication equipment that had been designed in the nineteen-thirties. Radios for vehicles were virtually inexistent. Tanks communicated with each other via coloured pennants, a method that was impractical in combat.

In 1941, the Red Army only had 43,000 radios and the war did not make matters any better, as out of the fifteen specialised factories, fourteen had been moved to the Urals and only began producing in quantity at the end of 1942. The great majority of radios made were for ground troops. Only 10% of tanks were equipped with radios and these were always command tanks.

This lack of communications equipment meant that all of the Soviets' efforts were ruined due to a lack of coordination. Reports and orders generally arrived too late and the Germans could quickly anticipate all of their enemy's movements.

Lend-Lease helped to turn the situation around as the Allies would supply a very large number of radios (245,000) and telephones.

"When my village was liberated, I went to the military commissary. I was immediately trained by the reserve regiment of the unit that had liberated us. However, we

Below.
12-RP model radio.

Left.
A soldier in the snow camouflage suit (see page 131) communicates with the UNA- J field phone, winter 1943.

SIGNALS EQUIPMENT

Model	Range in reception	Range in transmission	Network
4-A	150 kms	75 kms	division
5-TK 2	50 kms	25 kms	regiment
12-AK	150 kms	75 kms	division
6-PK 1 1	6-25 kms	5-8 kms	regiment-company
9-R	18-25 kms		vehicular
10-R	25-45		vehicular
71-TK	18-50 kms	18-30 kms	armour
72-TK	50 kms	25 kms	armour
12-RP	12-30 kms	6-15 kms	regiment
RB-38	12-35 kms	8-25 kms	battalion
Una-J & F *	300 m	300 m	platoon

(*) Field telephone

did not have enough time and I did not complete the Morse code training. I was attached to the 1028th Special Signals Regiment which worked for the General Staff of the 2nd Ukrainian Front. We were several women under the command of a Starshina who had fought in the Battle of Stalingrad."

Recollections of Issakova Olga Nicolaievna,
1028th Signals Regiment.

Right.
RB-38 radio.

MEDICAL SERVICES

At the time, medicine in the Soviet Union was free, but there was a catastrophic lack of doctors throughout the country. Although the Army managed to train medical personnel in peacetime, there were never enough medics, doctors, surgeons and specialists at the start of the mobilisation in 1941.

"I did my medical training in 1942 in the Urals and passed out with the rank of Mladchiy-Leitenant. I was attached to the 32nd Guards Division in 1943 as commander of its Medical Battalion. Our role was to pick up the wounded, give first aid, write the personal details on the wounded men's labels and evacuate them."

Recollections of Sabada Maria Sergeïnovna,
32nd Guards Division.

Above.
Evacuation of a soldier in September 1941. Rifles and blankets are used to fashion a stretcher.

Next, the sanitary transport evacuated the wounded towards specialised hospitals at the rear. The latter were divided into two categories according to the length of hospitalisation, more or less than 35 days.

"I acquired my first notions of first aid thanks to the Oso-viakhim. When war broke out, I underwent a crash course in medicine at Samarkand. Once these studies were completed, I was attached to field hospital 3261 as a surgeon. We had a huge amount of work and gangrene was a big cause of mortality with our wounded."

Recollections of Lukas Helena Constantinova,
Starschiy Voyenfeldsher, field hospital No 3261.

The medical battalion of an infantry division comprised of two medical officers for 31 political officers! To make up for the lack of doctors, students were rushed through their curriculum and assigned as fast as possible to the new units.

Another weak point was the lack of medication and modern equipment in field hospitals.

The medical services were structured in the following way: right up by the front lines, the mobile field hospitals dealt with triage and evacuation. They could treat and hold the lightly wounded in need of less than fifteen days of treatment.

Above.
A group of doctors and orderlies at a field hospital in 1942.

A list of wounded in field hospital No 2348, assigned to unit No 50,18 February 1945. In the columns from left to right are: Surname-name, year of birth, military speciality, exemption from service, nationality, Communist Party membership, unit, address. Signature of the colonel commanding the hospital.

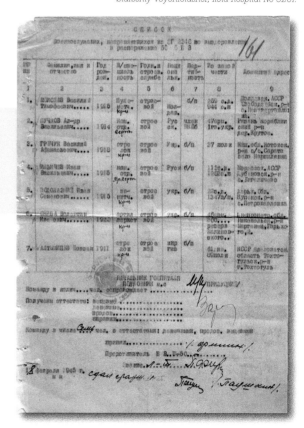

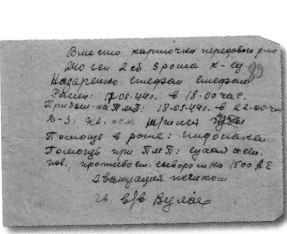

Left.
An evacuation label. It states that the soldier belongs to the 2d Infantry Battalion, 5th Company. He was wounded on 17 May 1944 at 18.00 hrs and arrived at the aid post on the 18th at 22.00 hrs. A bullet has penetrated the lower head and the lip needs to be stitched. The soldier can be evacuated on foot. Doctor's signature.

ENGINEERS

Engineer troops played an important role on the Eastern front. They were especially expert in river crossing operations and in field construction.

They also laid landmines as well as defused the enemy's. The role of these troops evolved and following Stalingrad, the Soviets formed assault engineer units, specially trained and equipped for urban combat. Using flame-throwers, the engineers paved the way for the infantry.

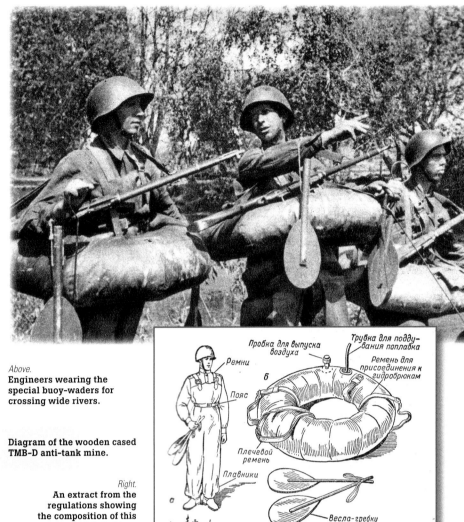

Above.
Engineers wearing the special buoy-waders for crossing wide rivers.

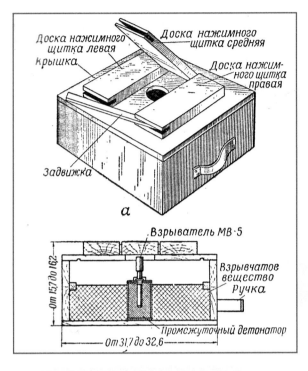

Diagram of the wooden cased PMD-6 antipersonnel mine.

Diagram of the wooden cased TMB-D anti-tank mine.

Right.
An extract from the regulations showing the composition of this special clothing.

Right.
An extract from the manual of field fortifications and trenches.

Below.
August 1942, army sappers are building a block against tanks with tree trunks and mines

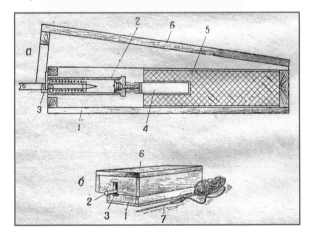

Below.
An extract from regulations showing mine laying.

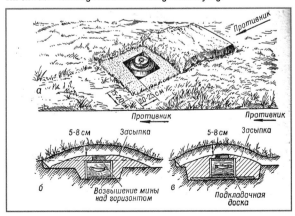

NKVD TROOPS

The NKVD (*Narodnyy Kommissariat Vnutrennikh Del*) or People's Commissariat for Internal Affairs was created on 10 July 1934.

Before this date it had been known under different names. The first of these was the *VCheKa* (Extraordinary Commission for Combating Counter-revolution and Sabotage), created on 20 December 1917. This political police was tasked with combating "enemies of the people" and controlling all aspects of Soviet life and watching over foreigners.

On 6 February 1922, it took the name of *GPU* (*Gosudarstvennoye Politischeskoye Upravlenie*) for State Political Directorate which became, on 15 November 1923, the OGPU (*Ob'edinennoe Gosudarstvennoe Politischeskoye Upravlenie*), or Joint State Political Directorate.

The NKVD comprised of several ministries:

★ The border-guards, whose mission it was to protect the 20,000 km of land borders and the 40,000 km of coastline.

★ The armed troops of the NKVD whose mission was one of internal security, re-establishing order and guarding sensitive areas.

★ State security, whose role was that of political control within the USSR.

★ Railway guards (*Konvoy*)

★ General directorate of *Gulag* (*Glavnoye upravlyeniye lagveryey*) prisoner camps.

The SMERCH or military counter-intelligence was created in 1942. Its mission was to "purify" the populations of previously German occupied territories, the interrogation of former POWs, and to crack-down on malingerers.

NKVD members had to be politically sure and were mostly recruited from children of Party members or the military.

This ministry was considerably strong, as its armed troops had undergone military training and were particularly well equipped.

They also carried out a military police role, guarding POWs, and looking for deserters and anti-Soviet partisans.

During the course of the war there were fifty-nine border guards regiments, forty-three NKVD divisions, three Konvoy divisions and fourteen various brigades. Some, transformed into infantry divisions, such as the 10th NKVD Division, fought with distinction in the defence of Stalingrad. It became the 181st Infantry Division on 5 February 1943.

The "blocking units" that appeared at the beginning of 1942 should also be mentioned. These were mostly made up of NKVD members and operated behind the front lines on the look out for stragglers and deserters. Any military personnel who appeared to be shirking from duty were arrested and, at best, sent to a punishment battalion, or otherwise to the Gulag after a quick trial.

These units were created following Stalin's 28 July 1942 order No 227 which was published in *Pravda* the next day. Its message to Soviet soldiers was that they could not retreat another step.

"It is easy to criticize this order 65 years after the events. However, at the time, it was our last chance to halt desertions, and to hope to win the war. Today, it should be recognised that these orders were a real success and that there were less desertions."

Recollections of Lieutenant
Kravchenko Vladislav Nikolaievitch, 199th Infantry Division

A little known unit, the NKVD Special Brigade, was formed in Moscow on 27 June 1941. It was tasked with behind the lines sabotage missions, reconnaissance and helping partisans, under the direct control of the High Command.

Above.
NKVD troops Leitenant of the State Security Department. These officers are recognisable by their collar tabs: although the colours remain those of the NKVD (brick-red background with raspberry piping), there is also a silver rank emblem in the centre, represented here by a star. The man has the pre-military Voroshilov sharpshooter badge. The collar of the M.35 tunic has silver piping.

The pay book of Starschiy Serzhant Onorine Guermane Yakolevitch, of the 166th NKVD Regiment, tasked with guarding strategically important industries.

THE MILITIA

Beginning 25 June 1941, it was decided to mobilise Party members, Komsomols and workers battalions in order to create militias (*Opolcheniye*). They were formed at military district level and mostly in the large industrial centres, such as Moscow, Leningrad, Kiev, Stalingrad and Odessa.

As a general rule, all citizens aged between 16 and 60 for men, and 18 to 50 years of age for women, were conscripted. A lot of these had served with the Osoviakhim, which prepared them for civil defence duties against air raids, for anti-aircraft defence and assignment to the medical services.

The NKVD also formed the *Istrebitelnyi* (security battalions) whose role was to guard factories and other sensitive areas. Made up of men and women, up to 1,755 of these have been counted.

It is estimated that the number of mobilised militia members numbered four million by the end of 1941, allowing for the creation of 30 militia divisions. However, they were often badly trained and equipped, which led to very heavy losses at the front.

For propaganda reasons, some militia units were equipped with weapons made by their comrades who had remained behind at the factory. For example, the Stalingrad Tank Brigade, created on 4 February 1941 with steel workers, was fitted out with tanks that came directly from their own factory's assembly lines.

Some militia units fought with distinction and were transformed into regular infantry units. The 2nd Leningrad Militia Division, formed in July 1941, became, on 23 September 1941, the 85th Infantry Division. Its artillery regiment was equipped with guns that came straight from the Kirov factory.

Below.
NKVD Honour badge (1940-1946).

Below.
The pay book of private Zaveglov Leonid Petrovitch, a machine-gunner with the 7th Border Guards Regiment. He saw action at Leningrad before being transferred to the 36th Guards Division and sent to Stalingrad. Zaveglov ended the war being decorated with the Order of Glory 3rd class, the Medal for Bravery, the Medal for the Defence of Leningrad, Stalingrad and the Capture of Budapest, and the Victory over Germany. During the war, he was wounded seven times and concussed twice.

PARTISANS

On 3 July 1941, Stalin gave his first speech since the German invasion. He ordered the creation of partisan units in the occupied territories. These groups carried out a guerrilla war against the enemy, blowing up bridges, destroying roads and fuel tanks.

The Partisans were all under the command of Marshal Voroshilov. However, well before the war, the Party had set up an organisation for this type of action and trained leaders to achieve this end.

"As a member of the Komsomols, I went into the forests as soon as the Germans arrived. We had already made stores of food, weapons and ammunition. We numbered around a hundred. I was a scout with the Zhukov Detachment and I hid my Ppsh 41 under my civilian clothes. Early in the evening on 5 November 1942, we attacked a German post. Approaching the canteen, I began crawling and I threw a grenade inside. Just after, I was hit by a bullet at the top of my thigh. My comrades dragged me along, but they had to hide me under the snow. 24 hours after, they came back to look for me. My wounds were treated immediately, but as there were complications, a plane came and took me to Moscow. A surgeon amputated my leg and I was next sent to Central Asia to convalesce. I was awarded the Partisan Medal Second Class for my actions."

Recollections of Antonina Yakovlievna
Figlovskaya, Zhukov Detachment.

The strength of partisan units varied. They were autonomous and looked after themselves. The largest units were given orders from Moscow via radio. Units were organised as follows: *Stonia* were small units, a 200 to 400 man battalion was called *Otriad*, a regiment *Polk*, and a division *Divisia*.

Life as a partisan was very tough and these units carried out an inhuman war. Any prisoners taken were systematically executed, as they could not be kept around. The German command was forced to mobilise large numbers of soldiers to combat the partisan threat.

"In 1943 I was 17 years old and I joined the Pojasky Partisan Brigade, where I was a scout. I was armed with a hunting rifle for this role. We fought against the Germans until the Red Army arrived. I was then integrated into the 90th Guards Division as a sniper. In 1944 I was wounded in the right leg by a shell splinter and spent eight months convalescing in hospital. After, I was sent to an artillery school where I passed out as section chief of a 76 mm gun. With the war against the Germans over, we moved off to fight the Japanese, but the war ended before we got there."

Recollections of Constantin Sergueïvitch Sasa.
Partisan with the Pojasky Brigade then the 90th Guards Division.

Below.
Partisan Medal 2nd class certificate.

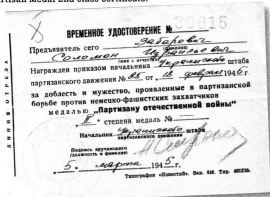

Partisan related objects: Kovpak bust, commander of a Partisan Division and Hero of the Soviet Union, bark *Lapki* sandals, TM-38 anti-tank mine, hand-crafted ring and belt, a filed down German belt buckle bearing an engraved star, Partisan Medals and certificate.

Right.
A female partisan of the Kovpak Division in March 1943.

Partisan Medals 1st and 2nd class.

Partisans placing explosives on a bridge, December 1943.

Pay book belonging to Mladshiy Serzhant Senacha Nicolaï Levonovitch. He served with the Parkhomenko Partisan Detachment, Brigade No 161, from 23 October 1943 to 28 June 1944 before joining the 31st Infantry Regiment on 27 July 1944. His partisan service is mentioned in the pay book. Senacha then served as a gun layer in a mortar unit. He ended the war with the Medal for Bravery.

ARM-OF-SERVICE INSIGNIA, 1935-43

Two periods can be distinguished: from 1935 to 1943, and after 1943, when shoulder boards were reinstated in the Red Army.

The Red Army personnel's arm-of-service was indicated, between 1935 and 1943, by the colours visible on collar tabs for all ranks, on the piping of officer's blouses, breeches and side-caps, and the colours visible on peaked caps and Budienovkas.

As can be seen on the table page 39, all arms of service had different colour combinations, save for artillery and armour who shared the same.

Further identification was ensured by a metallic device on the collar tabs, always in gold colour, except for veterinarians who had a silver badge to differentiate them from the medical service. Some of these devices could be pinned on collar tabs for a different arm of service. For instance, and more often in the case of pioneers, signallers, pontoniers, sappers and vehicle drivers, their metal device could be pinned on infantry, artillery, engineers (page 111), armour (page 125) etc. collar tabs to further indicate their trade. Despite the existence of a specific device for the infantry (target and crossed rifles, fig. 1), it should be remembered that this was unofficial.

On 1 August 1941, order 251 stipulated that the collar tabs and rank insignia for all arms would be army green. Order 261 of the following 3 August stated that the Gymnastierka tunic and breeches would be without piping.

METALLIC ARM-OF-SERVICE INSIGNIA ON COLLAR TABS

1. Infantry
2. Cavalry
3. Armour
4. Artillery
5. Engineers
6. Pioneers
7. Pontoniers
8. Railway troops
9. Electro-mechanical engineers
10. Signals
11. Transportation
12. Technical troops
13. Quartermaster, 1st type, to 30 March 1942
14. Quartermaster, 2d type, as of 1st Avril 1942.
15. Chemical warfare
16. Medical Service
17. Veterinary Service
18. Military Justice
19. Musicians
20. Air Forces
(Author's photo)

Below.
This Infantry Mladshiy Serzhant's blouse has the 1940 model collar tabs, with red middle stripe.

ARM-OF-SERVICE COLOURS, 1935-43

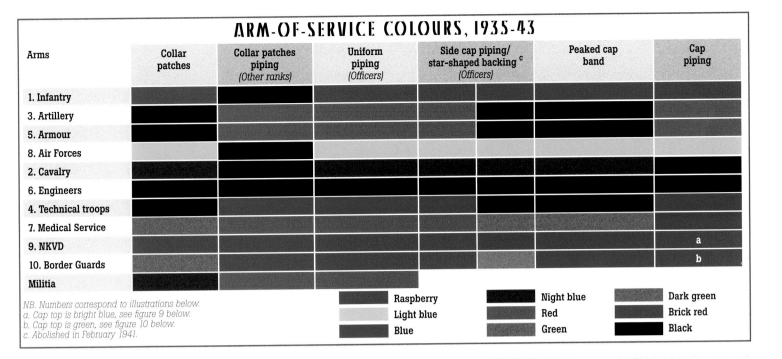

Arms	Collar patches	Collar patches piping (Other ranks)	Uniform piping (Officers)	Side cap piping/star-shaped backing c (Officers)	Peaked cap band	Cap piping
1. Infantry						
3. Artillery						
5. Armour						
8. Air Forces						
2. Cavalry						
6. Engineers						
4. Technical troops						
7. Medical Service						
9. NKVD						a
10. Border Guards						b
Militia						

NB. Numbers correspond to illustrations below.
a. Cap top is bright blue, see figure 9 below.
b. Cap top is green, see figure 10 below.
c. Abolished in February 1941.

Legend:
- Raspberry
- Light blue
- Blue
- Night blue
- Red
- Green
- Dark green
- Brick red
- Black

A **B**

ARM-OF-SERVICE COLOURS, 1935-43

A. As seen on the cloth backing to the star badge on the Budienovka winter cap (see also pages 56-57), and officers' side caps (see also page 52).

1. Infantry
2. Cavalry
3. Artillery
4. Technical troops
5. Armour
6. Engineers
7. Medical service
8. Air Forces
9. NKVD uniformed troops
10. Border Guards
11. State Security

B. As seen on caps and collar tabs (rectangular for the Gymnastierka and lozenge shaped for the greatcoat).

Left.
Colourized picture of an engineers Starshiy Leitenant. The collar tabs have a black base, and gold braid for an officer.

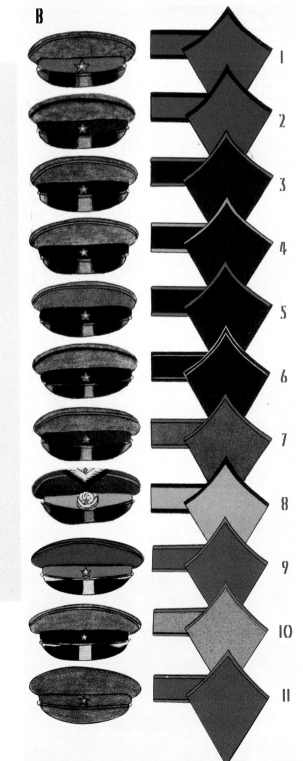

39

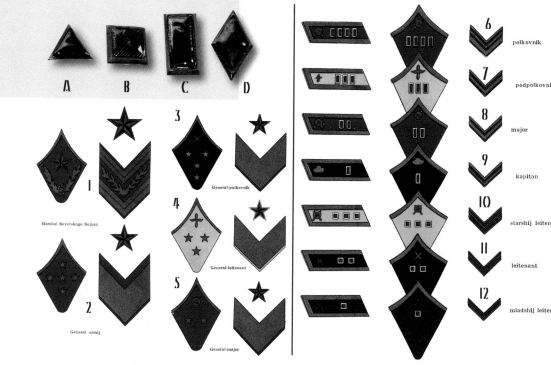

A B C D

Marshal Sovetskogo Sojuza
1

General armij
2

3
4
5

General-polkovnik
General-leitenant
General-major

polkovnik 6
podpolkovnik 7
major 8
kapitan 9
starshij leitenant 10
leitenant 11
mladshij leitenant 12

jefreitor 17
mladshij serzhant 16
serzhant 15
starshij serzhant 14
starshina 13

Between 1935 and 1943, rank was identified by geometrically shaped enamelled insignia on the collar tabs, and by sleeve stripes for officers.

On 1 August 1941, order 251 decreed the deleting of sleeve rank badges for troops in field dress.

ENAMELLED RANK INSIGNIA ON COLLAR TABS
A. NCOs.
B. Subalterns
C. Field grade officers
D. General officers

RANK INSIGNIA

ARMY GENERALS AND MARSHALS, 1940-43
(Sleeves: gold braid chevrons under embroidered star)
1. Marshal Sovietskovo Soyuza (Marshal of the Soviet Union)
2. General-Armii (Army General)

GENERALS, 1940-43
3. General-Polkovnik (Colonel-General)
4. General-Leitenant (Lieutenant-General)
5. General Major (Major-General)

FIELD GRADE OFFICERS
(Left: Gymnastierka, centre: greatcoat)
6. Polkovnik (Colonel)
7. Podpolkovnik (Lieutenant-Colonel)
8. Mayor (Major)
9. Kapitan (Captain)

SUBALTERNS
10. Starshiy Leitenant (Senior Lieutenant)
11. Leitenant (Lieutenant)
12. Mladshiy Leitenant (Junior Lieutenant)

NCOS AND PRIVATES
Note: 1940 pattern insignia with red middle stripe and yellow triangle.
13. Starshina (Sergeant Major)
14. Starshiy Serzhant (Senior Sergeant)
15. Serzhant (Junior Sergeant)
16. Mladshiy Serzhant (Senior Corporal)
17. Yefreïtor (Corporal)
The Krasnoarmieyets (Red Army man/ private) wore no rank insignia.

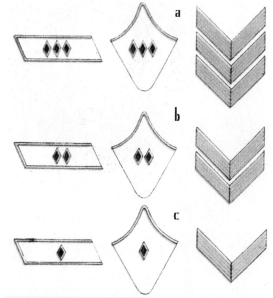

a
b
c

GENERAL OFFICERS, 1935-40
(collar tabs are in the arm of service colours)
a. Komkor (army corps commander)
b. Komdiv (division commander)
c. Kombrig (brigade commander)

Left.
Major-General Sokolov and commissar Riapoussov in May 1942.

Right.
This photo of a technical troops Polkovnik shows the collar and sleeve rank insignia.

OFFICER CADETS COLLAR TABS

Left.
This infantry school cadet is recognisable by his collar tabs. The photo was taken in Smolensk on 2 March 1942.

Below.
Engineer school cadets. The letters are the abbreviation of the school and arm of service. Photo dated 20 January 1941, at Borissov.

★ ◇◇◇◇	☆	Armeiskij komissar I-go ranga
◇◇◇◇	★	Armeiskij komissar II-go ranga
◇◇◇	★	Korpusnyj komissar
◇◇	★	Divizionnyj kommissar
◇	★	Brigadnyj komissar
□□□	★	Polkovoj komissar
□□	★	Bataljonnyj komissar
□	★	Starshyj politruk
□□□	★	Politruk
□□	★	Mladshij politruk
△△△△	★	Zamestitelj politruka

Above.
An Artillery school cadet.

POLITICAL OFFICERS

Collar tabs (other ranks pattern, in the colours of the parent unit) and sleeve insignia for the political officers corps.

Above right.
The other ranks model collar tabs can be clearly seen in this photo of a junior Politruk, as well as the sleeve star badge (see page 46).

Left.
This Starshiy Politruk wears a decoration that was somewhat rare for the time, the Order of Lenin.

NKVD TROOPS

Collar tabs and sleeve insignia for NKVD troops.

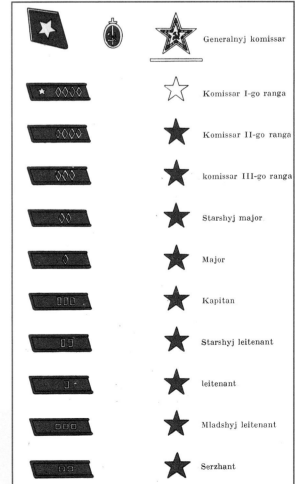

★	⬤	★	Generalnyj komissar
★ ◇◇◇◇		☆	Komissar I-go ranga
◇◇◇◇		★	Komissar II-go ranga
◇◇◇		★	komissar III-go ranga
◇◇		★	Starshyj major
◇		★	Major
□□□		★	Kapitan
□□		★	Starshyj leitenant
□		★	leitenant
□□□		★	Mladshyj leitenant
□□		★	Serzhant

RANK INSIGNIA, 1943-45

Beginning on 15 January 1943, order No 25 re-established shoulder boards for rank and arm-of-service identification.

From now on, rank was shown by metallic stars, and stripes, on the shoulder boards, and the arm of service by the coloured piping. Shoulder boards for the service/dress uniform were in gold colour (lace underlay, rank stars and metallic arm-of-service device) for combatant troops, and silver (lace underlay and stars) for non-combatant troops. Officers with the military justice, veterinary and medical services had narrower silver shoulder boards. The field uniform boards were in brown wool for combatant troops and greenish wool for non-combatants.

Shoulder boards were either removable, thanks to a buttoned undertab slid into a loop on the shoulder, or stitched permanently at the shoulder seam (greatcoat).

Metallic rank stars for shoulder boards. The large star was for field grade officers and the small type for subalterns. Stars were silver for non-combatant troops.
(Author's photo)

Right.
This Starshiy Leitenant wears the new shoulder boards. He has been awarded the Order of the Red Star. On the reverse of the photo is written, *Boris, town of Proskurov 1945.*

OFFICER SHOULDER BOARDS

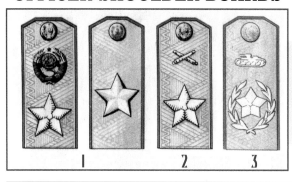

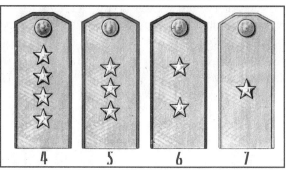

ARMY GENERALS AND MARSHALS

1. Marshal Sovietskovo Soyuza (Marshal of the Soviet Union)
2. Marshal Voisk (Artillery)
3. Glavniy Marshal (Armour)
4. General-Armii (Army General)

GENERALS

5. General-Polkovnik (General-Colonel)
6. General-Leitenant (Lieutenant-General)
7. General-Major (Major-General)

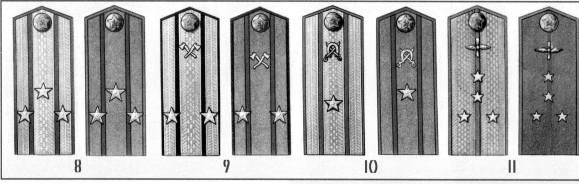

FIELD GRADE OFFICERS

(Left, service dress; right, field uniform)
8. Polkovnik (Colonel)
9. Podpolkovnik (Lieutenant-Colonel)
10. Mayor (Major)
11. Kapitan (Captain)

SUBALTERNS

12. Starshiy Leitenant (Senior Lieutenant)
13. Leitenant (Lieutenant)
14. Mladshiy Leitenant (Junior Lieutenant)

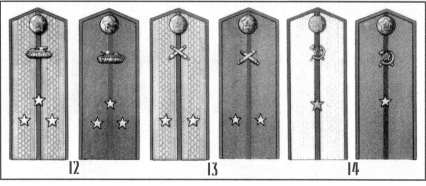

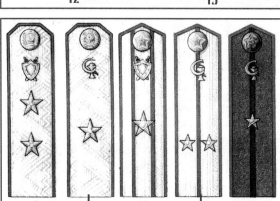

MILITARY JUSTICE, MEDICAL SERVICE AND VETERINARIANS

A. General-Leitenant (military justice)
B. General Major (medical)
C. Polkovnik
D. Leitenant (veterinarian)
E. Mladshiy Leitenant.

This Leitenant wears the silver narrower shoulder boards of medical officers. He has been awarded the Order of the Red Star.

ARM-OF-SERVICE COLOURS, OFFICERS' UNIFORMS, 1943-45

ARMS	SHOULDER BOARDS FIELD DRESS			SHOULDER BOARDS SERVICE DRESS/FULL DRESS			PEAKED CAP		
	Piping	Stripes	Underlay	Piping	Stripes	Underlay	Top	Piping	Band
Infantry									
Artillery									
Armour									
Air Forces									
Cavalry									
Engineers									
Technical troops									
Medical Service									
NKVD									
Border Guards									

Note on officers' shoulder boards and parade tunic badges:
★ *Combatant troops: shoulder boards with a gold underlay, arm-of-service device and rank stars.*
★ *Non-combatant troops: shoulder boards with a white/silver underlay, arm-of-service device and rank stars. The parade tunic's sleeve and collar braid were also silver (see page 73).*
★ *Military Justice, Medical and Veterinary service: narrow silver lace shoulder boards, gold arm-of-service insignia (except for veterinarians) and rank stars. The sleeve and collar braid on the parade tunic were also gold coloured.*

ARM OF SERVICE COLOURS, NCOS AND OTHER RANKS, 1943-45

ARMS	SHOULDER BOARDS FIELD DRESS		SHOULDER BOARDS FULL DRESS		PEAKED CAP		
	Piping	Underlay	Piping	Underlay	Top	Piping	Band
Infantry							
Artillery							
Armour							
Air Forces							
Cavalry							
Engineers							
Technical troops							
Medical Service							
NKVD							
Border Guards							
Militia							

Raspberry
Bright blue
Light blue
Blue
Night blue
Red
Green
Dark green
Garnet
Brick red
Golden yellow
Black
Brown-green

Right.
This colourized studio portrait of an infantry Leitenant's shows the golden yellow shoulder boards and his Order of the Red Star.

This Kapitan wears a Kittel adorned with a ribbon bar showing the Order of the Red flag and the medal for War merit. The lozenge badge is an unidentified Academy badge introduced in 1946. The soft shoulder boards are the M.43 pattern, with a single stripe down their length, the rank stars are the small size for subalterns. He is shod with felt and leather officer boots (see page 79).

SHOULDER BOARDS, 1943-45

OTHER RANKS

(Left, service dress; right, field dress)

1. Starshina (Sergeant Major)
2. Starshiy Serzhant (Senior Sergeant)
3. Serzhant (Sergeant)
4. Mladshiy Serzhant (Senior Corporal)
5. Yefreïtor (Corporal)
6. Krasnoarmieyets (Red Army man)

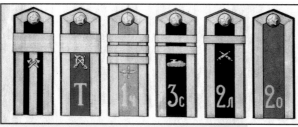

OFFICER CADETS

Left.
Flying school officer cadet.

Right.
This officer cadet is easily recognisable by his shoulder boards. He has been awarded the Order of the Great Patriotic War, the Medal for Bravery, the Guards Badge and Artillery Badge.

OTHER RANKS

1. Officer cadet in an artillery school
2. Infantry, field dress, removable boards, lend-lease manufacture
3. Artillery, field dress, removable boards
4 and 5. Infantry, field dress, sewn on the greatcoat
6. Infantry, parade dress, sewn on the greatcoat
7. Engineers, field dress, removable boards
8. Air forces, parade dress, removable boards
9 and 10. NKVD, parade dress, removable boards.

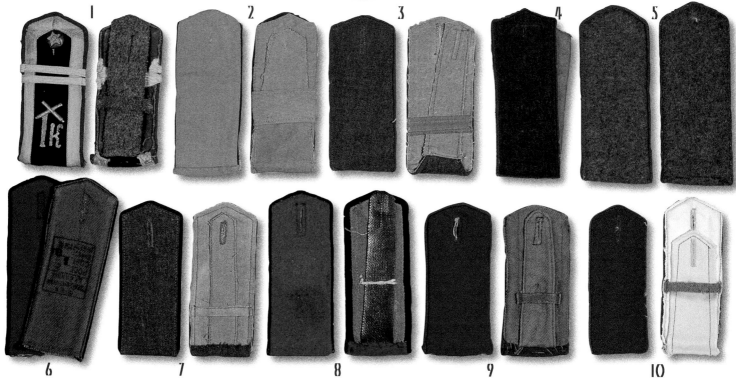

Greatcoat collar tabs (all ranks) for parade and field dress are adorned with a large uniform button (see page 71).

NCOS, REMOVABLE BOARDS

NCO rank stripes are garnet for field dress and yellow (plain braid or metallic) for service/full dress (gold arm-of-service device) in the case of combat troops. For non-combat troops, stripes are white for all uniforms, with silver arm-of-service device.

Photo of Serzhant Semen Ulianov Nikolas. The NCO stripes can be seen on the field uniform shoulder boards. He has been awarded the Order of the Great Patriotic War, the Anti-Aircraft Defence Badge and the Medal for the Defence of Stalingrad.

11. NKVD Yefreïtor, parade dress
12. Artillery Serzhant, parade dress
13. Quartermaster troops Serzhant, parade dress
14. NKVD Serzhant, parade dress
15. Pioneers *Yefreïtor*. The stripes were cut from an infantry officer's shoulder board, the undertab has been made with a piece of Waffen-SS camouflage material!
16. Infantry Serzhant, field dress
17. Artillery Serzhant, field dress
18. Medical Serzhant, Baltic fleet Naval infantry, parade dress
19. Artillery Starchiy Serzhant, parade dress
20. Armoured corps Starchina, field dress.

SUBALTERNS

21. Artillery, field dress, removable board
22. Armoured corps, field dress, removable
23. Infantry Maldchyi Leitenant, parade dress, removable.

FIELD GRADE OFFICERS

24. Infantry Kapitan, parade dress, removable board
25. Field dress, removable, no arm of service device.
26 and 27. Infantry Major, field dress, removable
28. Major, technical troops (silver backing) with the infantry, embroidered rank star. Parade dress, removable.
29. Infantry Major, parade dress, removable.
30. Air forces technical troops Podpolkovnik (silver backing), parade dress
31. NKVD troops (bevel-edged board) Major, field dress.

Parade dress shoulder board for an artillery signaller. In order to stiffen the board, the unit tailor or individual soldier has added an oblong piece of metal inside.

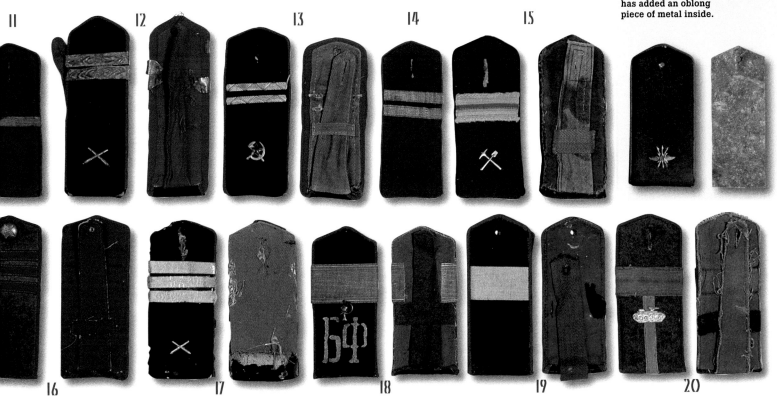

VARIOUS INSIGNIA

There were very few cloth or embroidered insignia within the Red Army. These are mostly found during the 1935-43 period.

Air Force

On the left sleeve:
★ embroidered pilot's wings that came into use on 8 August 1924 with order No 1030
★ mechanic's badge, introduced on 6 November 1925 following order No 1097. Order No 23 of 26 January 1942 saw the introduction of sleeve insignia for engineer-technicians.

These sleeve insignia were abolished by order No 25 of 15 January 1943 (the same one that brought in the wearing of shoulder boards).

Political officers

Since September 1935, the corps of Political officers had worn an embroidered red star, with a hammer and sickle in the centre, on the lower sleeve. Worn on both the Gymnastierka and the greatcoat, these stars were deleted in August 1941.

NKVD

NKVD State Security were characterised by an embroidered insignia sewn on the arm. This oval-shaped badge had a silver wire border with an embroidered gold wire sword, hammer and sickle in its centre. These sleeve badges were also abolished by order No 25 of 15 January 1943.

Above.
A photo of three pilots, wearing 'French' type tunics with the pilot's wings on the left sleeve.

Illustration of the pilot's sleeve insignia.

Right.
These political officers wear their specific badge on the greatcoat sleeves.

Political Commissar sleeve insignia.

NKVD troops sleeve insignia.

Anti-tank artillery

On 1 July 1942, order No 0528 introduced a special badge for by anti-tank artillery personnel. Worn at the top of the left sleeve. The cannons could be embroidered, printed with coloured molten rubber, or metallic. This insignia was officially abolished for officers on 30 June 1955 by order No 105 and for NCOs and privates on 4 August 1956 by order No 120.

Wound stripes

Wound stripes were introduced on 14 July 1942, by order No 213. From that point on, any wounded member of the military was given a wound certificate and stripe upon leaving hospital. Red stripes were for serious wounds and yellow for slight wounds. The wound stripes were always sewn above the right blouse pocket, having been

Above.
Two members of an anti-tank unit. The insignia on the left sleeve is the printed type.

Top left.
The anti-tank artillery badge. The base is black with red piping, the colour of the artillery. Top. Embroidered variant for officers. Bottom. Printed insignia for other ranks.

Left.
This artillery Leitenant has been wounded several times, the last being a slight wound (yellow stripe).

attached to a piece of backing cloth beforehand, even for a single stripe.

A stripe was awarded for as many times as the soldier was wounded, and always in a chronological fashion.

Brassards

★ The road traffic personnel brassard appeared in 1941. It was a red coloured brassard with a black circle in which was placed a white letter Π.

It also existed in badge form, like that for the anti-tank artillery.

★ The armband for guard detail commanders was red with the letters КH (*Nachalnik Karaula* = guard commander). It was only worn with the combat or service uniform.

Above.
Armband for personnel on military police duties (the initials meaning 'War patrol').

Right.
Germany 1945. This guard commander wears the regulation armband. Also note the leather leggings.

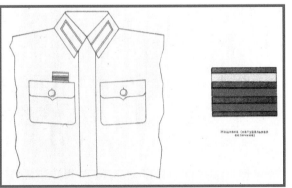

Left.
Plate showing the wound stripes and where they were placed on the blouse.

Even today, little is known about the Red Army and myths and clichés abound. These preconceived ideas are largely due to the image portrayed by the German propaganda following Operation Barbarossa.

MODEL 1936 HELMET

Indeed, the German propaganda services tried to portray the Soviet soldier in the light of their racial and political prejudices.

Photographers focused mostly on the racial diversity of the prisoners and only showed obsolete materiel. Anything that showed the superiority of the German race and soldier was used.

However, as the war in the East evolved, so did the image of the Soviet soldier. An explanation to the defeats suffered, beginning in 1943, led the Germans to belatedly portray the Frontovik as a determined, tenacious and well equipped combatant.

But, although the uniforms and equipment of the Red Army Soldier had improved, they had always been of a very good standard. To our Western eyes, this equipment may appear rough, but it was very straightforward, whilst, at the same time, functional and robust.

In the following chapters, dealing with the uniforms and equipment used during the Great Patriotic War, a great number of previously unpublished period photos are shown. For the years 1935-43, a large number of studio and portrait photos exist. Indeed, the possession of a camera was something that

On this German propaganda-oriented picture, these Soviet prisoners are wearing the M.36 steel helmet (foreground) and the M.40 (background). The greatcoats are devoid of any insignia. *(ECPAD France)*

had to be declared and very few soldiers could afford to own one. Soldiers, therefore, called upon professional photographers or kept their military identity photograph as a souvenir.

From 1943 onwards, the Soviet soldiers captured more and more prisoners, and had access to German war trophy cameras, leading, therefore, to a multitude of photos showing the everyday life. The only problem is that photos showing equipment, vehicles and planes were forbidden and generally taken in a hurry, or at an angle that does not allow for accurate identification.

The photos were processed by civilian studios in liberated territories, or officially by units that used photography such as air aerial reconnaissance squadrons.

As for press photographs, they were used for Party propaganda purposes. They always portray the Soviet soldier wearing his side cap in order to show his invulnerability, contrary to the German soldier, always shown wearing his helmet.

HEADWEAR

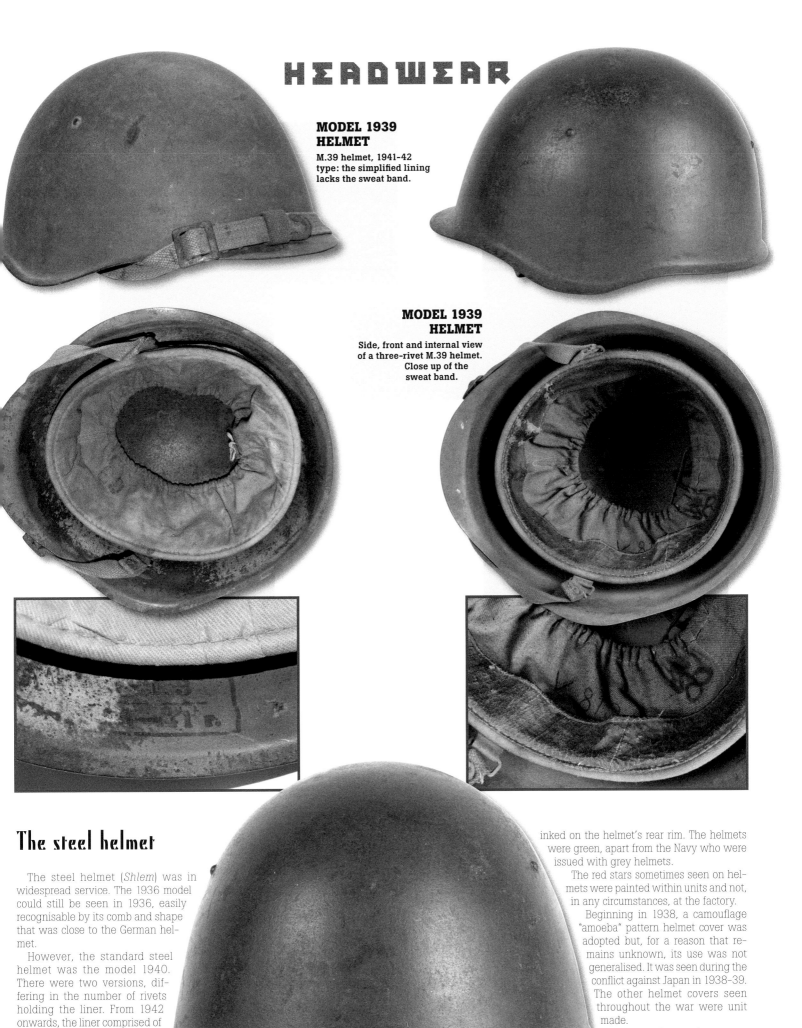

MODEL 1939 HELMET

M.39 helmet, 1941-42 type: the simplified lining lacks the sweat band.

MODEL 1939 HELMET

Side, front and internal view of a three-rivet M.39 helmet. Close up of the sweat band.

The steel helmet

The steel helmet (*Shlem*) was in widespread service. The 1936 model could still be seen in 1936, easily recognisable by its comb and shape that was close to the German helmet.

However, the standard steel helmet was the model 1940. There were two versions, differing in the number of rivets holding the liner. From 1942 onwards, the liner comprised of three pads held in place by six exterior rivets. The web chin strap was held by a rivet on each side. Markings were inked on the helmet's rear rim. The helmets were green, apart from the Navy who were issued with grey helmets.

The red stars sometimes seen on helmets were painted within units and not, in any circumstances, at the factory.

Beginning in 1938, a camouflage "amoeba" pattern helmet cover was adopted but, for a reason that remains unknown, its use was not generalised. It was seen during the conflict against Japan in 1938-39. The other helmet covers seen throughout the war were unit made.

Using paint or other means to camouflage helmets was not in widespread use, except for white in the winter.

49

Another M.39 helmet with lighter paint. Close up of the markings: the year of manufacture, factory and size. This helmet was made in Leningrad, 1940.

Six-rivet M.40 helmet manufactured in 1944.

This M.40 six-river helmet has been whitewashed.

Right.
Side and interior view of another six-rivet M.40 helmet.

The Pilotka

The side cap (*Pilotka*) was made of light green canvas. Its shape has hardly changed to this day. A green enamelled or painted tin star was worn at the front. The officer's side cap had piping, as well as a small fabric star in the colour of the arm (deleted in February 1941, see table on page 39), upon which a small red enamelled star was affixed. 1941 saw the appearance of a brown wool winter side cap.

Above.
A selection of other ranks side caps, note the variations in colour.

Right.
A fairly typical way of wearing the side cap by this Krasnoarmieyets in 1945.

Infantry officer side cap, made in 1939.

Infantry officer side cap without the cloth star behind the metal insignia (after February 1941).

THE GREY UNIFORM FOR OFFICERS IN THE ARMOURED CORPS

On 3 December 1935, order No 176 from the USSR Defence commissariat introduced for armoured corps officers a new uniform in a distinctive grey colour. All uniform elements would be grey, with a red arm of service piping: side cap, service cap, Gymnastierka, trousers, breeches and greatcoat (see also page 118). But only the M.43 field blouse and breeches were made up to the war's end.

Right.
**Tank officer side cap, made in 1938.
As per regulations, it is cut from grey cloth.**

OFFICER SIDE CAPS

**Side cap for an artillery
officer. Dated 1937, it is
devoid of coloured backing
for the enamelled star.**

Right.
**Cavalry officer
side cap.**

Bottom.
**A flying school cadet.
The side cap is an officer's
model. Note the officer
cadet belt buckle. The photo
is dated 22 June 1941.**

Left.
**Field service officer side cap.
The coloured backing for
the star badge is absent but
outlined by stitches.
The sweatband is
in tan leather.**

Right.
**Pilotka for an air force
officer; close up of
the markings and 1940 date.**

The service cap

The peaked service cap (*Furajka*) was made of khaki canvas or brown wool, with a black chin strap held by two small brass uniform buttons, and a black pressed cardboard peak. The interior had a sweatband.

The wool cap featured a coloured crown, band and piping [1].

The cap band bore an enamelled star, or a tin green painted version for khaki field caps.

The 1924 pattern service cap was higher, the top was lined with canvas overall, the sweatband was made from whitish canvas. The leather peak, brown coloured underneath, was short and rounded.

1935 Pattern service caps have a lower top, with a partial grey cloth lining. The sweatband is made from a leather substitute. the pressed cardboard peak is wider and slightly square-shaped, as a duck bill. Both sides are black or brown-green.

Service caps were the same pattern for all ranks, except those for generals, who had higher quality caps.

The field cap, entirely made from khaki cotton canvas, was issued to all ranks, without distinction of arm or service.

1. See tables on pages 39 and 43.

M.1924 SERVICE CAP

Engineers M.24 cap, note the canvas lining.

M.1935 SERVICE CAP

Infantry M.35 cap and interior markings.

Below.
This photo allows us to see the distinctive shape of the M.35 cap.

Right.
A period picture of the M.24 cap with large version star.

Below.
Medical services M.35 cap (green band, red piping). Note the metal eyelets on the side of the top.

M.1935 SERVICE CAPS

M.1935 service cap in the raspberry red infantry colours, details of the inside markings.

Below.
Another M.1935 service cap in infantry colours

Right.
M.35 Artillery cap: black band, red piping.

Right.
M.1935 pattern cap for the cavalry: blue band, black piping.

The peak of this cap is army green. This was common practice up to the nineteen-forties.

THE FIELD UNIFORM CAP

The khaki canvas cap for the field uniform, much liked by officers.

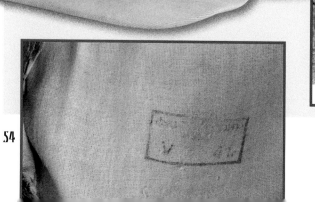

Kapitan Ossiev, Hero of the Soviet Union, wearing the field uniform cap.

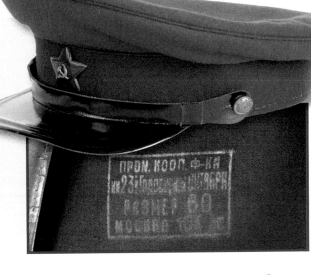

Three NKVD caps:
blue top, brick red
band, raspberry red piping

Right.
This tank Starshiy leitenant
has another variant of
service cap. He wears
the 1943 modified M.35
tunic and has been
awarded twice with the
Order of the Red Star.

Below.
Border Guards cap:
green top, blue band,
raspberry red pipings.

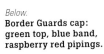

Right.
Plate showing the shape
of the field uniform cap.

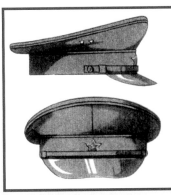

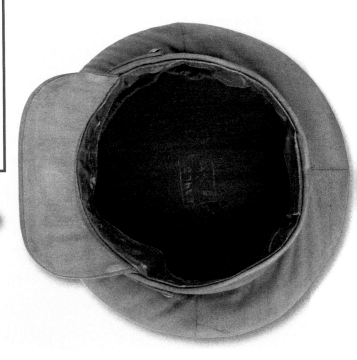

The Budionovka

The Budionovka hat was brought into service by General Budyenny. Initially it was a cloth winter cap with earflaps retained by buttons. A canvas summer version without earflaps came along next and was nicknamed "hello-goodbye."

The front bore a large cloth star in the arm of service colour (see page 39), upon which was attached a red enamelled or green painted star.

The M.19 cap had a fairly high point, the M.22 had a less pronounced point and leather tabs to secure the earflaps. The M.27 had canvas buttoning tabs.

M.19 infantry Budionovka.

Right.
This soldier wearing the pre-war Excellent soldier badge (inset) has the M.27 Budionovka.

M.19 cavalry Budionovka.

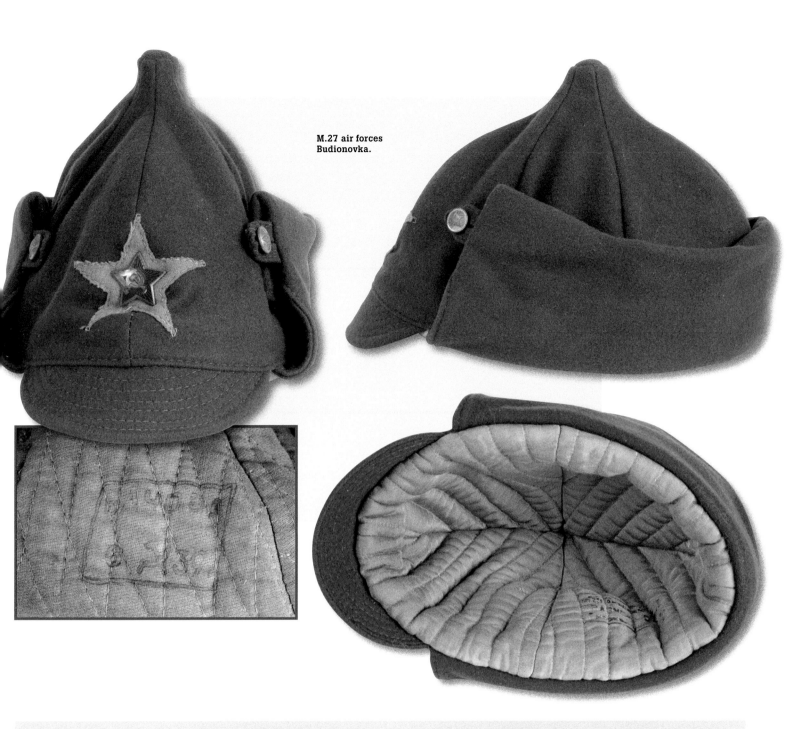

M.27 air forces
Budionovka.

The Panama hat

The Panama was a canvas hat with a cloth chin strap, it had the same insignia as the Budionovka bonnet. The lining was made of red cloth.

The Panama was only issued to troops operating in hot regions (the Caucasus, Manchuria and Mongolia…)

On this 1939-dated picture, these infantrymen are wearing the Panama hat, including the commissar at right. The latter wears a raincoat with his specific badge on the sleeves.

The Shapka-Ushanka

The Shapka-Ushanka was adopted on 5 April 1940 by order No 18 in order to replace the Budionovka. This was a brown-green coloured synthetic fur hat with two flaps to protect the ears and the nape of the neck. The officers' Shapka was made of sheepskin or astrakhan.

Several variants of the Shapka-Ushanka.

White fur officer's Shapka-Ushanka.
The stamped tin star is painted green.

Right.
This Politruk wears a round shaped Shapka-Ushanka.

58

Left.
A square shaped Shapka-Ushanka worn with the Polushubok fleece coat (see page 78)

Right.
Astrakhan Shapka-Ushanka.

Above.
Official illustration of the Shapka-Ushanka.

The Finka was a flat fur cap reserved for officers.

Below.
This photo of a group of officers in Leningrad in 1942 shows us a great variety of headwear: a Budionovka and Shapka-Ushankas in various materials.

The Papasha

The Papasha was an astrakhan hat reserved for generals and marshals at the beginning of the war. However it was authorised for wear from the rank of colonel upwards in 1943.

For generals, its crown was red with a gold cross, and the badge was an enamelled star in a circle; for colonels, the crown was green with gold wire, the enamelled star was plain.

Above.
The female soldier's beret.

The Female beret

The felt, or wool M. 41 beret, was exclusively reserved for female personnel and was of a brown-green or blue colour. The front bore a green enamelled or painted tin star. Note that female personnel also frequently wore other regulation headwear: Budionovka, cap, side cap and Ushanka.

Left.
A Shapka-Ushanka for this Krasnoarmieyets.

Below.
Side caps for all these medical service personnel.

Below.
Female officers wearing the brown wool beret. One is very faded.

Headwear stars

The enamelled stars for service caps were 38 mm in diameter for officers and 34 mm for other ranks. The side cap stars were 24 mm.

Between 1936 and 1939, the badge was made in two parts, the star itself and the hammer and sickle.

Stamped metallic stars, painted green or red, appeared in 1941.

1 and 2. 1936 pattern cap stars.
3 and 4. 1939 pattern cap stars.
5. Red painted tin star.
6 and 7. 1939 pattern star for the *Pilotka* side cap.
(Photos by the author and F. Coune)

Above.
1936 pattern star on a NKVD cap.

Below.
A Budionovka for this Starshiy leitenant.

Above.
Smaller 1939 star on this Air Forces Budionovka.

1939 pattern star on field uniform caps. It was common practice to slide the chin strap over the badge to hold it in place.

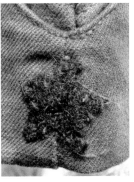

Above.
Cut out cloth star.

Right.
Red painted star. The arm-of-service coloured star backing was abolished in February 1941.

Green painted stars.

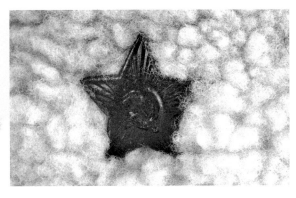

UNIFORMS
THE GYMNASTIERKA

A traditional garment of Eastern European countries, the tunic was an integral part of the image of the Russian, then Soviet soldier.

The military origins of this garment date back to the end of the 18th century. The tunic was, at this time, reserved for exercise or carrying out chores when in barracks.

It then progressively became part of the summer field uniform. During the course of the Russo-Japanese war, the tunics were dyed green as the white colour was too visible. It was then generalised to become an all season field uniform garment starting in 1912.

The Gymnastierka of the First World War had two breast poc-

M.29 TUNIC

A cotton 1929 pattern tunic. It is recognisable by its three visible buttons. The breast pockets were 12.5 cm wide and 13.5 cm high. The garment has 1935 pattern infantry collar tabs (raspberry background, black piping, enamelled insignia), as well as a triangular rank badge for NCOs.

The collar is made in three sections and on the right we can see the stitching joining the sides to the rear. Also note the typical placing of the collar tabs, specific to the M.29 tunics, as well as the reverse of the rank badge and arm of service insignia, both of which are metallic.

kets. A buttoned slit on the left side of the neck allowed it to be put on. It had a standing collar and the shoulder boards could be removable or permanently sewn-on.

As soon as the Bolsheviks took power, they quickly abolished the shoulder boards, but retained the tunic as it was. Its shape then underwent a few modifications, up to the model adopted in 1935, which included:

★ According to order No 628 of 8 April 1919: standing collar, two lower pockets, sleeve cuffs with two buttons; fly-fronted chest opening

★ Order No 322 of 31 January 1922: fold down collar

★ Order No 419 of 27 February 1923: buttons stamped with the symbol of the Soviet Union (hammer and sickle on a star-shaped background)

★ Order No 702 of 30 May 1924: two breast pockets, lower pockets deleted

★ Order No 190 of 19 April 1929: there were now a cotton "summer" tunic and a cloth "winter" patter. The buttons of the chest opening were visible once again.

THE M.35 TUNIC

Order No 176 of 3 December 1935 determined the shape of the new tunic, but also the new rank insignia, worn on the collar tabs, and at the base of the sleeves for officers (see page 39).

The other ranks tunic

It had two patch breast pockets, 12.5 cm wide and 15.5 cm high. The neck opening was fly-fronted, the sleeves secured by a cuff with two small buttons and the elbows were reinforced. The collar was closed by one or two small metal hooks. The cut was rather loose and the hem reached as far as mid-thigh, thus offering extra protection against the cold.

A false white collar, sewn onto the collar with large stitches, prevented the early wear and tear of the tunic in this area. If the soldier did not have such a collar, he cut one out of a piece of white cloth.

Although the 1935 pattern tunic was standard, there were several specific variants:

★ for female personnel, the chest buttoning was the other way round.

★ medical personnel received with a tunic that had four exterior patch pockets.

★ in the case of marksmen, the strip hiding the buttons of the front opening was raspberry coloured.

EVOLUTION OF THE 1935 PATTERN

When war broke out in 1941, many of the tunics in service were the model 1929, due to the 1935 pattern being generalised slowly. The same applied to the rank insignia, which were modified again following order No 391 of 2 November 1940. Indeed, it is estimated that in 1941, 60% of military personnel still wore 1935 pattern rank insignia.

During the summer of 1941, following order 251 of 1 August, the tunics underwent a few modifications: deletion of sleeve rank insignia, coloured collar tabs and brass buttons. For all arms and services, the collar tabs, rank insignia and buttons were, in principle, a drab green. The reality was somewhat different, as many period photos show that very few drab green collar tabs were apparently made and worn even less. Officers kept their coloured collar tabs and other ranks tunics just had their collar tabs removed, except for NCOs.

M.35 TUNIC

M.35 tunic. The buttons of the chest opening are hidden by a strip of cloth. The collar tabs are the 1940 pattern in the infantry colours. The latter now have a red coloured central stripe. The tunic also has the Voroshilov Marksman Badge and the Red Army "Excellent soldier" badge. The rear view allows us to see the elbow reinforcing.

Right.
An infantryman with the M.35 tunic.

The collar is now made in two parts and still has four rows of stitching. The collar tabs were probably added on the production line. The rank insignia is still screw-backed; the reverse of the infantry badge shows a tin split-pin that pierces the cloth. This was a later production pattern, that was used on rank insignia as well.

Right.

M.35 tunic for privates and NCOs.

Гимнастерка

63

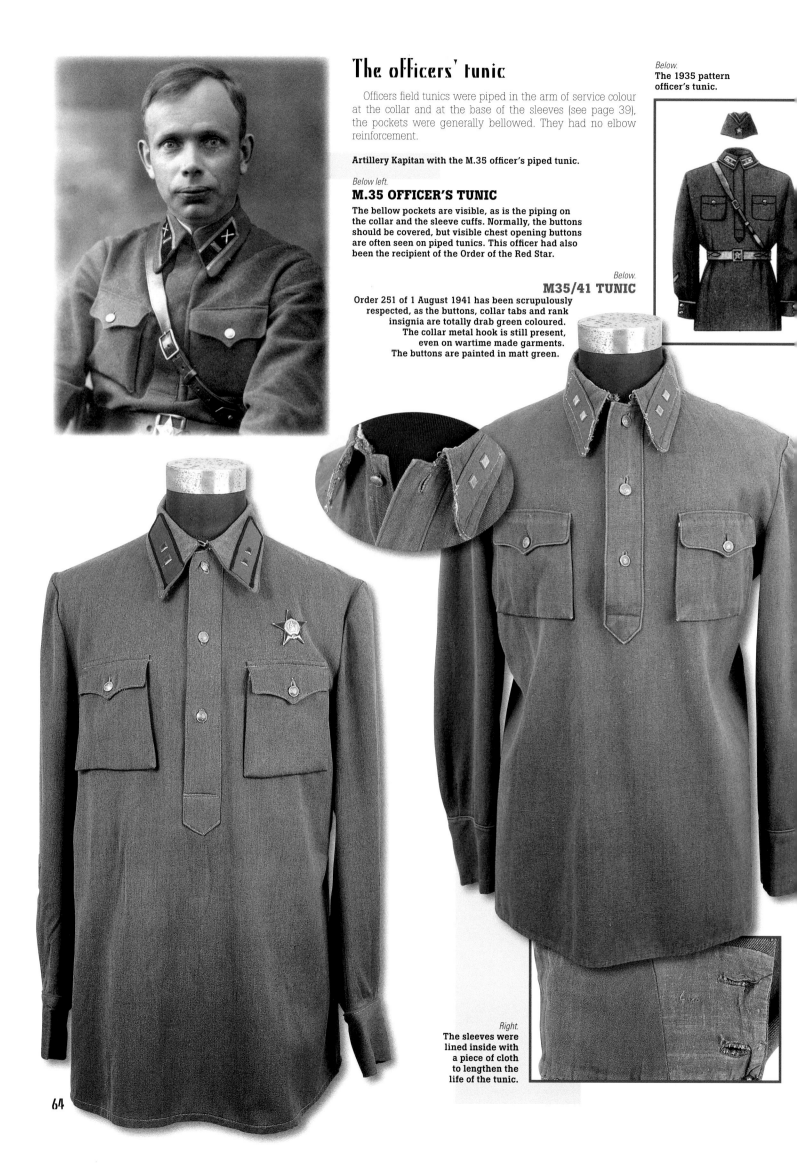

The officers' tunic

Officers field tunics were piped in the arm of service colour at the collar and at the base of the sleeves (see page 39), the pockets were generally bellowed. They had no elbow reinforcement.

Artillery Kapitan with the M.35 officer's piped tunic.

Below left.
M.35 OFFICER'S TUNIC

The bellow pockets are visible, as is the piping on the collar and the sleeve cuffs. Normally, the buttons should be covered, but visible chest opening buttons are often seen on piped tunics. This officer had also been the recipient of the Order of the Red Star.

Below.
M35/41 TUNIC

Order 251 of 1 August 1941 has been scrupulously respected, as the buttons, collar tabs and rank insignia are totally drab green coloured. The collar metal hook is still present, even on wartime made garments. The buttons are painted in matt green.

Below.
The 1935 pattern officer's tunic.

Right.
The sleeves were lined inside with a piece of cloth to lengthen the life of the tunic.

64

THE M.43 TUNIC

At the start of 1943, Stalin had understood the need to promote patriotism, the Slav Soul and Mother Russia, rather than faith in the Communist Party, to win the war. Among other measures, he brought back Tsarist era shoulder boards and modified the tunic with order 25 of 15 January 1943.

The Motherland was in danger, with fighting still in progress at Stalingrad and a large part of the Soviet Union still under German occupation. However, the appearance of this new tunic and its new rank insignia was a stroke of genius. The war in the East now became the Soviets' "Great Patriotic War"! At the same time, new decorations (Ushakov, Nakhimov) and orders (Kutuzov, Nevsky, Suvorov…) were created.

According to Stalin's directives, the new uniforms and shoulder boards (*Pogony*) would have to be issued to the entire Red Army between 1-15 February 1943!

The 1935/43 tunic

Whilst waiting for the 1943 tunic to be generalised, the model 1929 or 1935 tunics were fitted with either removable or stitched on shoulder boards. Although there is no official nomenclature, the latter tunic is commonly called the 1935/43 pattern. This model was worn until the end of the war and sometimes, even a few years after.

The 1943 pattern tunic

This tunic differed from the 1935 pattern by the appearance of a standing collar closed by two buttons. The chest opening was closed by three visible buttons. The cuffs were also closed

M.35/43 TUNIC

Left and above.
Whilst waiting for the new tunics to be issued, the 1935 pattern tunics were modified by adding shoulder boards.

by two buttons and elbow reinforcing was absent from the early production garments.

There were still two types of tunic, one for the summer in tan cotton, and the more commonly seen winter version made from green-brown combed wool.

Upon receiving the new tunic, the soldier was issued at the same time with a set of shoulder boards and two buttons for them, as well as three white false collars. This issue was entered in the service book (see pages 20-21).

M.43 TUNIC

It was made from thick cloth, the dye did not hold up very well to wear and washing. The collar was a standing type with visible buttons. The shoulder boards are the field pattern, on a drab green background, with red piping for artillery or tanks. Also seen here are the Medal for Combat Merit, Guards Insignia, Excellent Mortar Man Badge and above, two wound stripes (one severe and one light wound). The view of the back shows that the elbow reinforcements did not feature on the first production run tunics.

Above.
A close up of the shoulder board. Note the tear made when adding the button, and the sewn-on loop. Shoulder boards were made with off-cuts of fabric, as stipulated by the salvage regulations.

Below.
View of the lining added to the inside of the cuffs.

The other ranks' tunic

The other ranks' tunic was of a similar shape to the officer's model, but it did not have breast pockets, piping or elbow reinforcements. The first 1943 tunics did not have the small holes near the collar, through which the soldier threaded a lace holding the button of the shoulder boards. Because of this, the soldier had to punch the holes himself, which often ripped the fabric.

Also, the tunic did not feature the loops at the shoulders to hold the Pogony. Once again, the Soviet soldier had to use his sewing skills to add this loop, although some just went ahead and sewed the shoulder boards, with or without the lower tab, straight onto the tunic.

The standardisation of the tunic in the months that followed solved these problems. It now had button holes, or a square section of cloth onto which the button was sewn, and loops for the boards.

The 1943 other ranks tunic was cut from with green cloth, which faded with washing or when steamed for delousing. Because of the numerous manufacturers, there are many shades of green, ranging from light green, to brown, grey etc.

By carefully studying period photographs, one realises that from the beginning of 1945 onwards, tunics with breast pockets were issued to all personnel regardless of rank.

As with the 1935 tunic, there was a 1943 pattern for women soldiers. Buttoning on the female side, it had loops for shoulder board and pleats on the chest.

M. 43 FIELD UNIFORM SHOULDER BOARDS

1. Infantry shoulder boards, sewn at the shoulder (mint, uncut specimen, 1945-dated).
2. Infantry shoulder boards, with undertab, for a Mladchiy Serzhant.
3. Infantry shoulder boards, sewn at the shoulder, thick and stiff pattern.
4. Infantry shoulder boards, with undertab, 1943 dated.
5. Infantry shoulder boards, made from American-supplied cotton material.

The buttons were not always the regulation brass pattern embossed with the Soviet emblem, a great number of other buttons were used, in brass, tin (4-hole), bakelite and horn, civilian buttons and even captured German ones (see on page 71).

M.43 TUNIC

Another first type 1943 tunic which has retained its original colour. The buttons are made of brass and the garment bears the first type Medal for Bravery and the Defence of Stalingrad medal. The shoulder boards are the field uniform pattern, with raspberry red infantry piping. This tunic has elbow reinforcements.

Right.
This NCO wears an early M. 43 tunic without breast pockets. The buttons are tin.

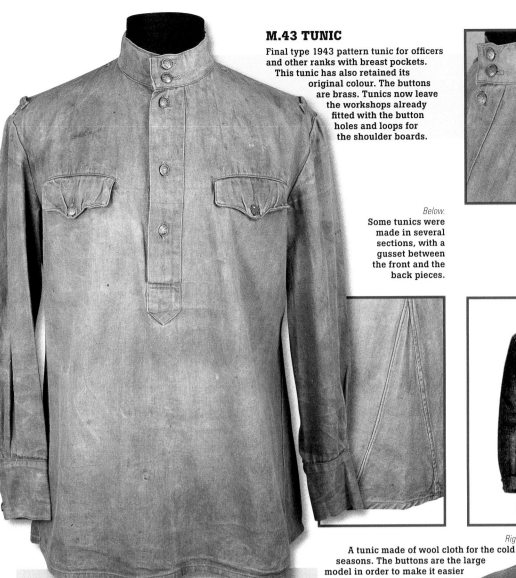

M.43 TUNIC

Final type 1943 pattern tunic for officers and other ranks with breast pockets. This tunic has also retained its original colour. The buttons are brass. Tunics now leave the workshops already fitted with the button holes and loops for the shoulder boards.

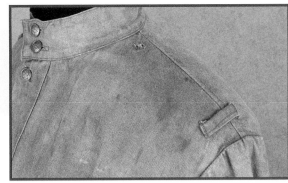

Below.
Some tunics were made in several sections, with a gusset between the front and the back pieces.

Below.
The 1943 pattern tunic for privates and NCOs.

A tunic made of wool cloth for the cold seasons. The buttons are the large model in order to make it easier to button up when the soldier is wearing gloves.

Right.

MARKINGS

Soviet tunics are very rarely dated. The ink markings are always found inside the garment near the hem, at the front or rear. With Model 35 tunics, markings indicate the year in its complete form (1939, 1940…) and generally include the name of the factory.

In the case of Model 43 tunics, the markings are in the shape of a square or rectangle, with the last two numbers of the year of manufacture followed by the letter "г" in Russian (г = g in our alphabet for goda = year), the size, indicated by a **P** followed by the numbers, 1, 2, 3 or 4. Sometimes there is only the factory name or the two first numbers 19…

Above, markings on a late-war ORs' tunic and, below, markings on woollen OR's breeches.

The officers' M. 43 tunic

It has two inside hanging breast pockets made of grey or white canvas, with only the buttoned flap showing. There are two holes at the base of the collar and a loop for attaching the shoulder boards.

Some tunics have piping in the arm of service colour on the upper edge of the cuffs.

The 1943 pattern officer's tunic.

MANUFACTURING THE UNIFORMS

Despite the problems encountered due to a large part of its territory being under occupation and the mobilisation of millions of men and women, the USSR managed to equip all of its military personnel.

The workshops mass produced the 1935 pattern tunic and other items of uniform, whilst all the time sticking scrupulously to the specifications. Therefore, if one looks at wartime made tunics, trousers, side caps etc., they are all very well made. It should not be forgotten either that twenty work camps manufactured uniforms throughout the war. Paradoxically, the prisoners of these camps were carried away on a tide of patriotism and freely worked at an infernal rate. It should also be mentioned that Lend-Lease played an important role, as the American and British allies supplied finished Red Army-pattern uniforms as well as millions of metres of cotton and wool cloth.

OFFICER'S M. 43 TUNIC

It has two breast pockets and arm of service piping in the colour on the cuffs. The wear and tear of this tunic makes the stitching patterns apparent. On the tunic are the Guards Insignia, two Medals for Bravery and the Medal for the Defence of Sebastopol. The field uniform shoulder boards are those of a lieutenant, on a drab green background. Shoulder boards for subalterns feature only a single middle stripe and smaller stars.

Below.
A close up of the raspberry red infantry piping.

Left.
A Starchiy Leitenant with the new 1943 tunic. The haircut is typical of Soviet troops.

Right.
This Mladchiy Leitenant has been issued with an other ranks' tunic without breast pockets.

AMERICAN MADE M. 43 TUNIC

It differs from the original pattern by its wide breast pockets and plain cuffs. The buttons, also American made, are green plastic.

Lend-Lease tunics

There were Soviet-manufactured tunics made with British or American-supplied materials, or tunics made by the Allies themselves. These are slightly better made, despite the fact that American manufacturers sometimes took liberties with the specifications (breast pockets, plain cuffs…).

The buttons are also American or British made and bear the names of the manufacturers, such as *RAB Co, Rex New Rochelle NY, Handy Button Mach. Co. Chicago…*

M. 1943 NKVD OFFICER'S TUNIC

This officer's (a Major) tunic has specific bellowed breast pockets. The shoulder boards are the field uniform pattern with a brown-green backing. Field grade officers have two middle stripes and larger stars. Also, note that the NKVD shoulder boards do not have pointed ends, but are angular in shape.

NKVD tunics

The first 1943 pattern tunics for NKVD personnel had the particularity of being made with breast pockets, as was the case with the 1935 pattern. The officers' pockets were bellowed. This detail disappeared with the standardisation of the tunic, but the NKVD troops still differed from the rest of the Red Army as they had shoulder boards with cut angles.

WEARING BADGES AND DECORATIONS

With the **1935 pattern** tunic, all insignia, medals, orders and so on, were displayed over the left pocket, except for the wound stripes introduced on 14 July 1942, which were sewn above the right pocket and always placed on a fabric backing.

With the **1943 pattern** tunic, **medals** were worn on the left and always in the following order of precedence: Gold Star of Hero of the Soviet Union, which was worn above the other medals and orders, next, closer to the neck opening, came the:
– Order of Lenin
– Order of the Red Banner
– Order of Glory, 1st, 2nd and 3rd class
– Medal for Bravery
– Ushakov Medal
– Medal for Combat Service
– Nakhimov Medal
– Partisans Medal 1st and 2nd class

– Medals for the defence of Leningrad, Moscow, Odessa, Sebastopol, Stalingrad, Kiev, Caucasus and the Trans-arctic
– Victory over Germany
– Victory over Japan
– Medals for the capture of Budapest, Königsberg, Vienna and Berlin
– Medals for the liberation of Belgrade, Warsaw and Prague
– Medal for labour during the Great Patriotic War.

The **orders** were worn on the right side, with the highest situated the closest to the front buttons. For example, the Order of the Red Star would have been as far right as possible, and the Order of Suvorov 1st class the closest to the buttons. The orders were worn in the following way:
★ Orders of Suvorov, Ushakov, Kutuzov, Nakhimov and Khmelnitsky 1st class
★ the same orders in their second class
★ Orders of Suvorov, Kutuzov and Khmelnitsky 3rd class

★ Order of Alexander Nevsky
★ Orders of the Great Patriotic War 1st class and 2nd class
★ Order of the Red Star

The Guards badge and that of excellent rifleman etc. were also worn on the right. If the tunic had pockets, the orders and badges were worn above them.

It should be mentioned that the wearing of pre-war badges such as those of the Osoviakhim (paramilitary defence organisation) was not permitted on the new 1943 pattern tunic.

All of the above is, of course, theoretical, as many period photos, or those taken after, show that the order of precedence was not strictly adhered to. Another common practice was attaching the Guards badge to the buttonhole of the right pocket, thus avoiding pushing the pin through the fabric.

69

OFFICERS' CLOTHING

The French

Early in the war, officers had a tunic known as the "French", with piping in the arm of service colour, introduced by order No176 on 3 December 1935.

It closed down the front with six large buttons and had four pockets and a fall collar.

Note that the name "French" referred to the British Great War General, Sir John French.

Left.
The French type officer's tunic with piping.

The Kittel

The Kittel was a service dress tunic adopted in 1943. It was closed by five buttons, had a standing collar and shoulder boards. The Kittel had piping in the arm of service colour and also existed in white cloth or canvas for the summer uniform.

The Kittel service dress tunic.

Below.
The coloured piping is clearly visible on the cuffs of this officer's Kittel.

Three officers in Sofia in 1944. The man in the centre has added shoulder boards to his Kittel. He wears the Order of the Red Banner and the Order of the Red Star.

The Plachtch

Officers had a grey gabardine *Plachtch* raincoat. It was closed by five buttons and had shoulder boards and collar tabs. It was tightened at the waist by a buttoned back belt.

Left.
This Kittel wearing officer has been awarded with the Order of the Red Star, first type Medal for Bravery and the Medal for the Defence of Stalingrad.

The grey gabardine officer's raincoat.

UNIFORM BUTTONS

16 MM TUNIC BUTTONS (POCKETS AND SLEEVES)

1 to 3. Brass
4. Steel
5. Aluminium
6. Black painted tin
7. Plastic
8. Tin
9. White tin
10. Aluminium
11. Bakelite
12 and 13. Front and reverse of steel and aluminium buttons
14. Pebbled zinc
15. Captured German button

18 MM BUTTONS FOR SHOULDER BOARDS

16. Tin buttons
17. Brass and steel
18. Painted steel
19. American made (also in green plastic)
20. Brass, domed shaped

22 MM BUTTONS FOR THE GREATCOAT AND ITS COLLAR TABS

21 and 22. Brass and tin

MISC. BUTTONS

23. Navy
24. Air Force
25. Technical and tank personnel
(Photo Militaria Magazine)

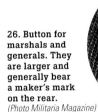

26. Button for marshals and generals. They are larger and generally bear a maker's mark on the rear.
(Photo Militaria Magazine)

26

Red Army uniforms had a great variety of buttons: brass, aluminium, steel, tin, leather, compressed cardboard, bakelite and plastic, of either Soviet or American manufacture, not forgetting salvaged civilian buttons, and German ones.

The uniform button was domed and stamped with the symbols of the Soviet Union: a pebbled star superimposed with a hammer and sickle in its centre.

This button was made of one or two parts. The reverse had a horseshoe-shaped ring which was sometimes removable.

Whatever the button was made of, order 251 of 1 August 1941 decreed that uniform buttons had to be painted green, but they are sometimes found painted black or grey, or sometimes just bare metal.

On the field tunic, collar, front opening, cuff and pocket buttons were 16 mm in diameter, and 18 mm for the shoulder boards.

For technical, air force and naval personnel, the button bore specific emblems: two crossed spanners for technical or tank personnel, wing and propeller for the air force and an anchor for the navy.

The uniforms of marshals and generals had larger buttons, with a design representing the eleven republics of the USSR.

PERIODICITY SCHEDULE FOR THE RENEWAL OF UNIFORMS AND EQUIPMENT

NCOS AND OTHER RANKS

Uniforms	Peace time	Wartime
Shapka	2 years	2 years [1]
Cotton side cap	1 year	2 years
Wool side cap	2 years	2 years [1]
Service cap	2 years	2 years
Greatcoat	3 years	3 years
Cotton blouse	6-8 months	6 months
Cotton breeches	6-8 months	6 months
Padded jacket	3 years	1 year [1]
Padded trousers	3 years	1 year [1]
Gloves	1 year	1 year [1]
Wool hood	1 year	1 year [1]
'Valenki' felt boots	3 years	3 years [1]
Leather boots	1 year	8-9 mo.
Ankle boots	1 year	8-9 mo.
Puttees	1 year	1 year

Equipment	Peace time	Wartime
Leather belt	4 years	4 years
Belt	2 years	2 years
Canvas suspension straps	4 years	4 years
Greatcoat strap	2 years	4 years
Haversack	4 years	5 years
Bread bag	4 years	5 years
Ten section	5 years	5 years
Mess tin	upon request	idem
Mess tin cover	4 years	4 years
Water bottle	upon request	idem
Water bottle cover	2 years	2 years
Leather pistol holster	6 years	5 years
Lanyard	4 years	5 years
Cartridge carriers	3 years	3 years
Bandoleer	4 years	4 years

OFFICERS

Uniforms	Peace time	Wartime
Service cap	2 years	3 years
Cotton side cap	1 year	2 years
Wool side cap	2 years	2 years
Shapka	4 years	4 years [1]
Cotton blouse	1 year	1 year
'French' tunic	2 years	3 years [2]
Kittel parade tunic	3 years	3 years
Cotton breeches	1 year	1 year
Blue wool breeches	3 years	3 years [2]
Fur vest	5 years	5 years
Leather boots	2 years	1 year
Polushubok fleece coat	3 years	3 years [1]
Padded jacket	3 years	3 years [1]
Padded trousers	3 years	3 years [1]
'Valenki' felt boots	3 years	3 years [1]
Leather gloves	3 years	3 years
Fur gloves	3 years	3 years

Equipment	Peace time	Wartime
Leather belt	5 years	5 years
Leather cross strap	5 years	5 years
Leather suspension straps	5 years	5 years
Leather pistol holster	10 years	10 years
Lanyard	4 years	4 years
Mess tin and cover	2 years	2 years
Water bottle and cover	2 years	2 years

1. Issue limited to front-line troops or to the cold regions.
2. Issue limited to rear area troops, to unit commanders and political officers.

THE MUNDIR PARADE TUNIC

Left.
A Leitenant wearing a Mundir with embroidered cuff tabs.

Right.
Mladshiy leitenant wearing a Mundir with silk woven cuff tabs.

The *Mundir* tunic was adopted late in the war as the parade uniform for all ranks. Made of dark green wool, it was closed by five buttons down the front.

The tunic was piped in the arm of service colour, which also appeared on the two oblong collar facings. These had a single gold stripe for NCOs, a single strip of braid for subalterns and two for senior officers. The officer's Mundir had cuff tabs in metallic wire, one for subalterns and two for senior officers. These tabs were in gold wire for combat arms and silver for technical troops.

There was also a double-breasted variant of the Mundir with two rows of buttons.

Left.
**Mundir for an infantry Frontovik: raspberry red piping and no collar facings or cuff tabs.
He is the recipient of the Order of the Red Star, the Guards badge and that of excellent machine gunner. His medals are for bravery in combat and for the defence of the Caucasus.**

Right.
Mundir of an Infantry colonel: raspberry red piping, gold coloured collar facings and cuff tabs for the combat arms. This officer has been awarded with two Orders of the Red Star, that for the Great Patriotic War, and the Guards badge. His medals are for Merit in combat, the defence of Moscow, the liberation of Prague, Victory over Germany, 30th anniversary of the Red Army and two Czech medals.

Left.
Mundir for a colonel of the technical troops in the artillery or armoured corps (red piping). The collar facings and cuff tabs are silver coloured for technical troops. This officer has earned the Orders of the Red star and the Great Patriotic war, and the badge of excellent tanker. He also wears the medals for victory over Germany, for the liberation of Prague, and for victorious labour.

The Mundir parade tunic.

MUNDIR TUNIC FACINGS

rank	sleeve	collar
Generals (marshals excepted)		
Field grade officers (services)		(Artillery)
Subalterns (combat arms)		(Air forces)
NCOs		(Cavalry)
Other ranks		(Engineers and Technical troops)

Above.
This officer wears the double-breasted Mundir.

Double-breasted Mundir for a NKVD Podpolkovnik. All the ornamentation is embroidered. The decorations are two Orders of the Red Banner, the Medal for Merit in combat and the Medal for the Defence of the Caucasus. On the right is the NKVD 15-year service badge. At the bottom are inscribed the initials for the Cheka and GPU.

Below.
A group of soldiers, with the two in the middle wearing the double-breasted Mundir.

Underclothes

For other ranks, they comprised of a collar-less shirt and long johns. These garments were white, with a summer version (cotton) and a winter version (cotton fleece).

Right.
The regulation shirt.

Left.
Front and rear view of the other ranks' breeches.
(Author's photos)

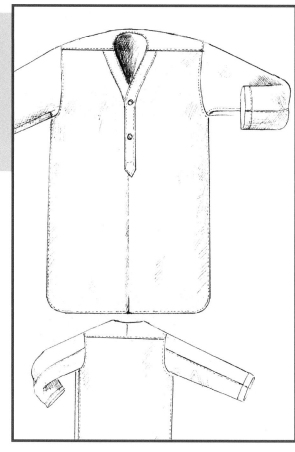

The breeches (*Charovari*) were made of cotton or wool. They were brown-green coloured with knee reinforcements, and were worn fairly high over the waist.

Their shape was rounded on the sides and they had laces at the leg cuffs to tighten the garment on the calves. These were worn with boots or ankle boots and puttees.

At the rear was a short tightening strap with a two-pronged metal buckle. The manufacturers markings were ink stamped at the inside rear, on the gusset piece.

NCOs had dark blue breeches without knee reinforcements.

Below.
A view of several other ranks' breeches.
(Author's photo)

Female personnel

The service uniform skirt (*Yubka*) was the 1938 pattern. Khaki or blue, it was mid-knee length.

The 1941 Pattern dress had a fold down collar (with collar tabs) and a waist belt. The 1943 pattern was similar, but with a standing collar and shoulder boards.

In the field, the skirt was replaced by male model breeches.

Берет

The 1941 Pattern skirt for female personnel, accompanied by a beret.

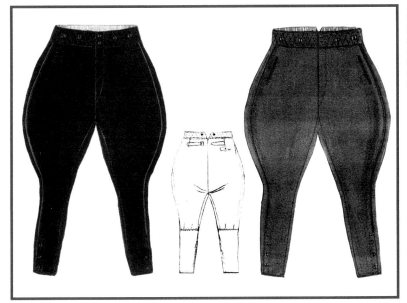

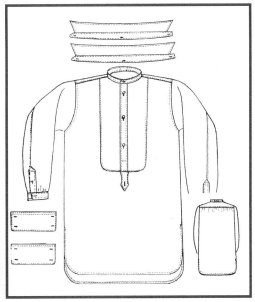

The officers' breeches, in blue cloth for service dress (left) and in brown-green material for field dress (right).

The officers' shirt was identical to the other ranks' pattern, but had removable collar and cuffs.

Officers' clothing

The service uniform officers' breeches were made of blue cloth with piping along the legs. The brown-green coloured field uniform model was identical, but did not have knee reinforcements and was sometimes without piping. These were worn with boots.

The straight leg officers' service uniform trousers (*Galife*) had piping in the arm of service colour. They were worn with shoes.

Officers' breeches in blue cloth.
(Author's photo)

Below.
Several pairs of officers' breeches.
(Author's photo)

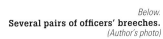

77

COATS AND GREATCOATS

OTHER RANKS' GREATCOAT

These two soldiers of a transportation unit wear the M.35 greatcoat, with pointed cuffs and triangular collar tabs.

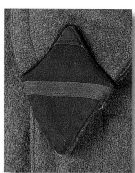

The 1935 pattern greatcoat closes down the front with four hooks and eyes. The Pattern 1940 collar patches bear a horizontal stripe. On the specimen shown, the top part of the lozenge, which should be in gilt for NCOs, is rendered with a piece of raspberry red braid. This particular greatcoat has been made with lend-lease brown wool cloth. The regulation grey wool greatcoat is illustrated on page 122.

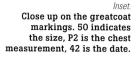

Inset.
Close up on the greatcoat markings. 50 indicates the size, P2 is the chest measurement, 42 is the date.

This Frontovik, very much reminiscent of the Tsarist period, wears a field cap and the M.43 greatcoat with buttons on the collar tabs. Photo dated 26 March 1945.

Right.
The M.43 greatcoat for other ranks had shoulder boards, oblong collar tabs with button and straight turn-back cuffs

All ranks were issued with a greatcoat (*Shinel*) made of heavy greyish coloured wool. It was very long and it was left to the individual to cut the skirt off depending on his size. The sleeves covered half of the hand.

It had two pockets and was closed with hooks. The back had a belt adjusted by two large buttons. The lining was made of green canvas and it had a single pocket.

The 1935 pattern greatcoat had pointed turn-back cuffs and collar tabs in the arm of service colour. The 1943 pattern greatcoat was characterised by straight cuffs and shoulder tabs.

The 1935 pattern officer's greatcoat had two rows of four buttons, and five buttons for the 1943 pattern, the outside pockets had a flap.

Rank badges and shoulder boards worn with the coats and greatcoats are shown on pages 39-42.

OFFICERS' GREATCOATS

Kapitan Georg Grigorovitch Lorine wears the 1935 pattern double-breasted greatcoat for officers', with two rows of four buttons.

Right.
This officer wears a M.35 tunic and the M.43 greatcoat. Eastern Front, 27 April 1943.

Below.
Officers with the M.43 greatcoat. The man on the left is armed with a PPS.43.

Scouts Krivtsoune Nicolas and Berezhnoi Sergeï in Marizul village. They wear the other ranks' M.43 greatcoat. That of the NCO at right bears no collar tabs.

WINTER PADDED CLOTHING

The most common winter clothing was the padded suit, comprising of a padded jacket, trousers (*Vatni Charovari*), accompanied by compressed felt boots (see page 79) and the Chapka-Uchanka hat. The coat had a standing, or fold down collar, and was closed by five large buttons. The fly-fronted trousers had two pockets and laces for tightening the bottom of the legs (see pages 132-133 for an illustration of the padded suit)

The Tielogreïka padded jacket closes down the front with five brass uniform buttons, and the sleeves by a wooden button.

Other winter issue garments

A reversed hide *Polushubok* or *Shouba*, sheepskin coat was also issued for the winter.

The *Bouchlat* was a three-quarter length padded coat adopted in 1941, mostly issued to engineer or motorised troops.

The *Becheka* was a three-quarter length fur-lined coat reserved for officers.

Above.
Different types and colours of (*Roukavitsi, Pertchatki*) gloves and mittens.

Below.
Illustration showing gloves and mittens.

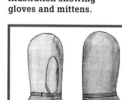

Above.
Regulation wool balaclavas.

The *Bouchlat* was double-breasted short coat cut from thick canvas: five button closure, buttoned cuff tabs and two belt hooks at the back.

Right.
The soldier at right armed with a Ppsh SMG wears the *Polushubok* sheepskin coat. There were many variations of colour.

BOOTS AND ANKLE BOOTS

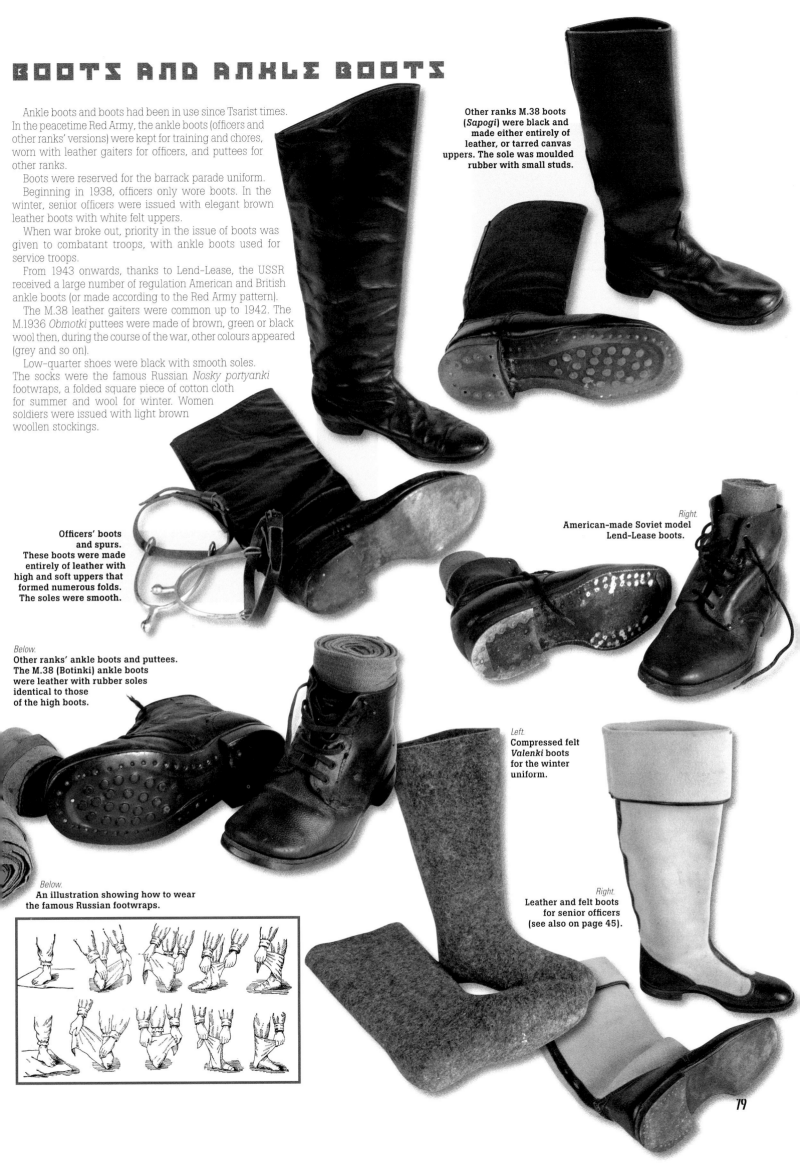

Ankle boots and boots had been in use since Tsarist times. In the peacetime Red Army, the ankle boots (officers and other ranks' versions) were kept for training and chores, worn with leather gaiters for officers, and puttees for other ranks.

Boots were reserved for the barrack parade uniform.

Beginning in 1938, officers only wore boots. In the winter, senior officers were issued with elegant brown leather boots with white felt uppers.

When war broke out, priority in the issue of boots was given to combatant troops, with ankle boots used for service troops.

From 1943 onwards, thanks to Lend-Lease, the USSR received a large number of regulation American and British ankle boots (or made according to the Red Army pattern).

The M.38 leather gaiters were common up to 1942. The M.1936 *Obmotki* puttees were made of brown, green or black wool then, during the course of the war, other colours appeared (grey and so on).

Low-quarter shoes were black with smooth soles. The socks were the famous Russian *Nosky portyanki* footwraps, a folded square piece of cotton cloth for summer and wool for winter. Women soldiers were issued with light brown woollen stockings.

Other ranks M.38 boots (*Sapogi*) were black and made either entirely of leather, or tarred canvas uppers. The sole was moulded rubber with small studs.

Officers' boots and spurs. These boots were made entirely of leather with high and soft uppers that formed numerous folds. The soles were smooth.

Below.
Other ranks' ankle boots and puttees. The M.38 (Botinki) ankle boots were leather with rubber soles identical to those of the high boots.

Right.
American-made Soviet model Lend-Lease boots.

Left.
Compressed felt *Valenki* boots for the winter uniform.

Below.
An illustration showing how to wear the famous Russian footwraps.

Right.
Leather and felt boots for senior officers (see also on page 45).

79

SPECIAL CLOTHING

Mechanised units personnel, such as tank crew members and drivers, wore blue overalls over the field uniform. These had a breast pocket on the left hand side and a thigh pocket on the right, as well as a belt. It was closed with either buttons, or a zip. However, a great variety of models and colours can be seen.

Tank crews were issued with a leather outfit comprising of a jacket and trousers. The short jacket was used by other ranks and lieutenants. A longer jacket was issued to officers from captain upwards (see also page 124 for an illustration of the tank crews leather uniform).

The jacket had two rows of four buttons. There were four pockets, two of which were patch pockets, and two false breast pockets.

The leather trousers had canvas cuffs at the base of the legs to ease the wearing of boots. They had two pockets, a back gusset and belt.

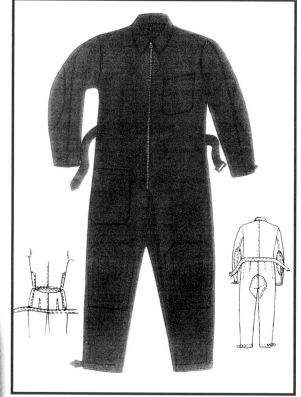

Right.
An illustration showing the overalls issued to motorised unit personnel. The model here is equipped with a zip.

The armoured troops leather uniform, jacket and trousers.

Right.
1942. These scouts wear the 'amoeba' type camouflage.

CAMOUFLAGE CLOTHING

Camouflage clothing was not only used by airborne troops. They were also issued mainly to scouts, assault pioneers and snipers.

1938 saw the appearance of the first camouflage uniforms during the war against the Japanese. The scheme chosen is known as 'amoeba,' but this is a name invented by collectors. This designates large, rounded patches similar to the shape of an amoeba seen under a microscope.

The 'summer' scheme displayed a green background printed with large black patches, whilst the 'autumn' scheme had a beige background with large brown patches.

The camouflage clothing consisted of two garments, the top was fairly large fitting with a hood

that covered the steel helmet and equipped with a veil to hide the face. Two side slits allowed the wearer to reach the equipment which was worn underneath.

The trousers were also large fitting with the leg bottoms tightened by a lace. A slit on each side allowed access to the breeches' pockets.

There were also overalls made of the same fabric (*Kombinezon Kamouflage*). As we have seen in the chapter concerning helmets, an 'amoeba' type helmet cover also appeared in 1938, but for reasons which remain unknown, it was never generalised.

1941 saw the appearance of a second pattern two-piece garment, upon which were sewn small clumps of artificial grass. It was almost identical in

design to the previous model, but did not include a veil and was equipped with integral gloves.

Towards 1943, another camouflage scheme appeared, of small white leaves on a grey-green background. During the course of 1944, the same scheme was used for an autumn version, by adding large brown patches.

1945 saw the introduction of the so-called 'saw-tooth' pattern. It was similar to the previous version, but the leaves were made up of numerous small squares. The autumn version was characterised

Right.
July 1944 at Narwa, Leningrad Front. These two scouts armed
with the PPSH.41 wear the 'amoeba' type camouflage.

by its brown patches, and the summer version by a yellowish
background.

It should be mentioned that these late patterns were mostly
seen on overalls.

Snow clothing

White clothing was introduced in 1940 following the war
with Finland. It comprised of a large robe with a hood and
integral gloves, with a nine-button frontal closure. It could be
adjusted via knotted drawstrings.

The end of 1941 saw the appearance of a new two-piece
white garment comprising of a white smock with two side pockets, trousers and a padded sleeveless vest. It had drawstrings
and integral gloves. This suit is illustrated on pages 123 and 131.

Below.
**1944. The scout on the right wears camouflage trousers with
the field blouse. Note also the M.40 combat knife on the belt.**

Below right.
**The artilleryman on the right wears the snow
robe. The mittens are held by strings.**
(B. Renoult collection)

Right.
**The first and second type snow camouflage garments
were used together up to the end of the war.
The helmets have been daubed with white paint.**

The end of 1941 saw the appearance of a new two-piece
white garment comprising of a white smock with two side pockets, trousers and a padded sleeveless vest. It had drawstrings
and integral gloves. This suit is illustrated on pages 123 and 131.

INDIVIDUAL EQUIPMENT

Although when the Red Army was created, most of the equipment was that of the Tsarist era, the Soviets innovated and produced straightforward equipment that was easy to manufacture, simple, and perfectly adapted to life in the field.

Leather equipment began to be phased out and replaced with cotton web, or canvas and leather. As was the case with armaments, the beginning of the war and the moving of factories, meant that there was a serious lack of equipment throughout 1942, but the Allies helped to in the supply of certain items.

Packs and backpacks

The model 1936 haversack was square-shaped and

Left.
M.36 backpack with the mess tin and its canvas cover, see also the soldier on page 101.

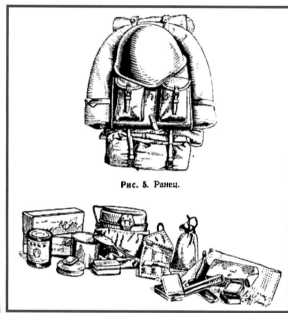

Рис. 5. Ранец.

Above.
This illustration shows the field equipment to which the M.39 haversack belonged. The top picture shows the tent/poncho *(Plaschch-palatka)*, rolled into a horseshoe shape. Below: combat rations, mess tin and cover, bags of flour and salt, personal hygiene items, tooth powder, tobacco pouch.

M.39 BACKPACK

M.39 backpack shown alongside the regulation shirt and long johns.

Left.
A collection of letters, just as they were carried in a Soviet soldier's pack. The way in which they are folded is characteristic of Russian post, note the Army Post Office number and the military censor's stamps.

1. Soap
2. Soap container
3. Toothbrush case
4. Tooth powder
5. Cup for rinsing the teeth
6. Shaving bowl
7. Razor and its case
8. Handmade comb

equipped with leather straps. The other ranks' version is recognisable by its straps placed at the top to attach the mess tin. The officers' model does not have this particularity.

The model 1939 haversack was made of canvas and had two outside pockets. The edges of the pocket flaps, as well as their closure straps, were brown leather.

The model 1941 haversack was only made during six months! It is identical in shape to the model 1939, but only the pocket closure straps are made of leather.

The model 1930 assault pack, or *Mieshok*, was inspired by the model 1910 Tsarist pack. It was a large canvas pouch with integral straps that are knotted at the top to close the pouch.

M.41 HAVERSACK

From left to right:
1. Butter container
2. Fat container
3. Shaving bowl
4. Handmade comb
5. Soap
6. Lighter
7. Miniature icon
8. Cigarette paper
9. Matches
10. Flour bag
11. Salt bag
12. Russian socks
13. Handmade matchbox cover
14. Chess game.

Right.
The model 1930 assault pack and the model 1941 bread bag, carried on the belt. See also on page 103.

Right.
This illustration shows the internal storage of the M.30 assault pack: from top to bottom, personal hygiene items, spare Russian socks, mess tin with its cover, combat rations.

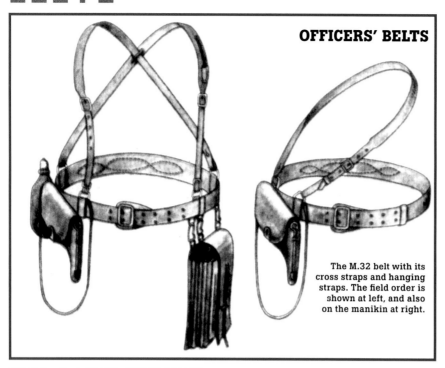

OFFICERS' BELTS

The M.32 belt with its cross straps and hanging straps. The field order is shown at left, and also on the manikin at right.

The officers' leather M.32 field equipment, front and back, with binoculars, map case, sidearm holster and whistle.

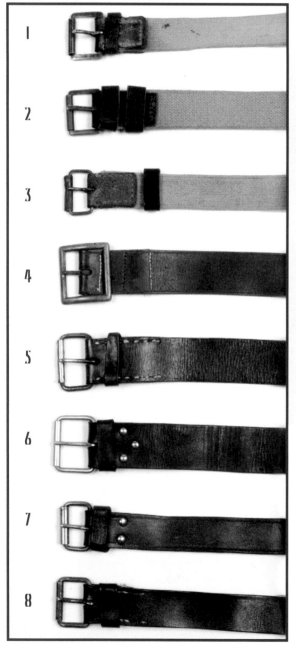

The other ranks' belt

The other ranks' belt (*Remenie*) was made of brown leather, with a pronged buckle and existed in various widths. The Americans supplied their obsolete 'Garrison belts,' a russet leather belt with a square single-pronged brass buckle. A canvas and lather belt appeared in 1938 and was generalised throughout the conflict.

1, 2 and 3. Leather belt strap.
4. American Lend-Lease belt.
5, 6, 7 and 8. Leather belt a single prong.

Officers' belts

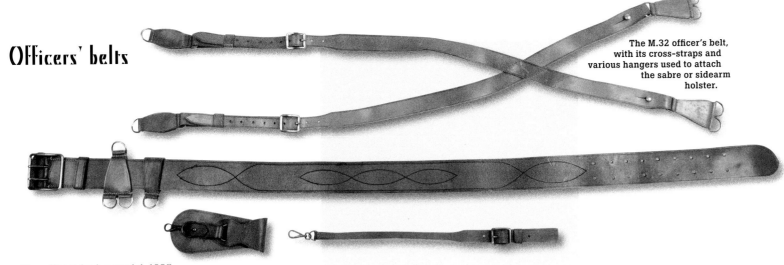

The M.32 officer's belt, with its cross-straps and various hangers used to attach the sabre or sidearm holster.

The officers had a model 1935 belt and cross strap made of fawn-coloured leather. The open buckle has a star stamped with the hammer and sickle. There were hangers to attach a side arm or sabre.

The model 1932 belt, also in fawn coloured leather, had a two prong buckle and two suspension straps that crossed over on the back.

MODEL 1932 BELTS

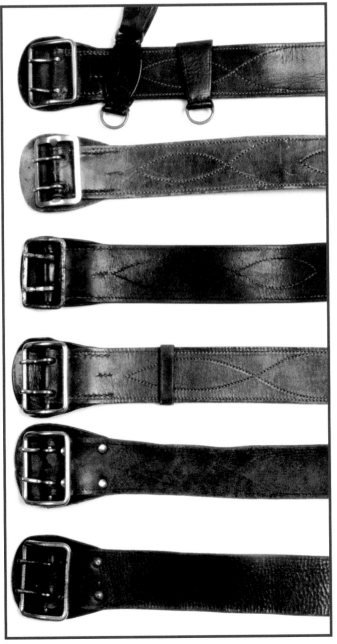

MODEL 1935 BELTS

AMMUNITION POUCHES

Above.
These three soldiers, armed with the Mosin rifle, are equipped with the Tsarist type ammunition pouches.

The rifle ammunition pouches (*Patrontach*) are the model 1937 version made of brown or black leather. They could carry four clips of five rounds. A ring placed at the rear was used to attach the hooks of the haversack straps.

As was the case of the belt, from 1938 onwards, leather and canvas ammunition pouches were made, identical in shape to the model 1937.

There was also an extra ammunition pouch, inspired by the model 1892.

The pouches for the SVT 40 automatic rifle were larger and made of brown leather. The early model had a ring at the rear. Wartime made pouches were made of poor quality leather and did not have a ring.

POUCHES FOR RIFLE AMMUNITION

1. M.1893 Tsarist ammunition pouch.
2-4. Various versions of the M.37 ammunition pouch for the Mosin rifle.
5. Baltic country made M.37 ammunition pouches for the Mosin rifle.
6. Leather and canvas M.37 ammunition pouches.
7. Extra canvas ammunition pouch for the Mosin rifle.

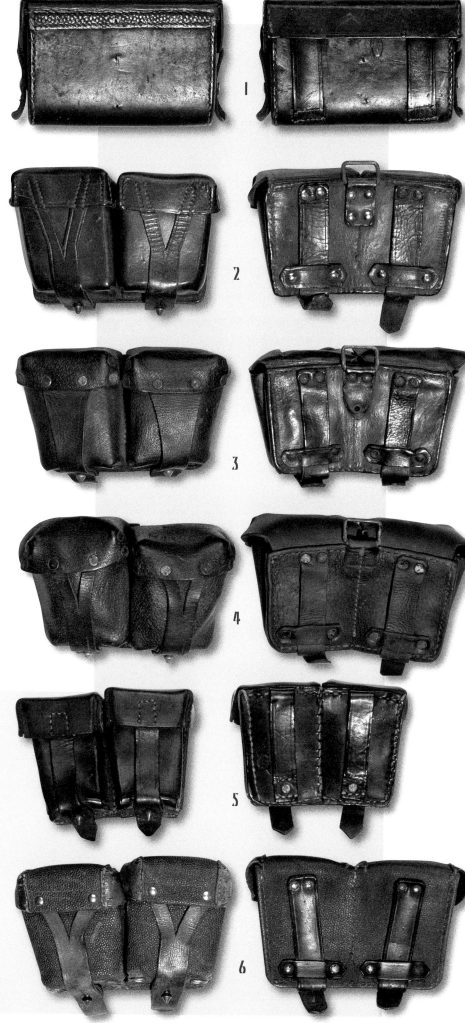

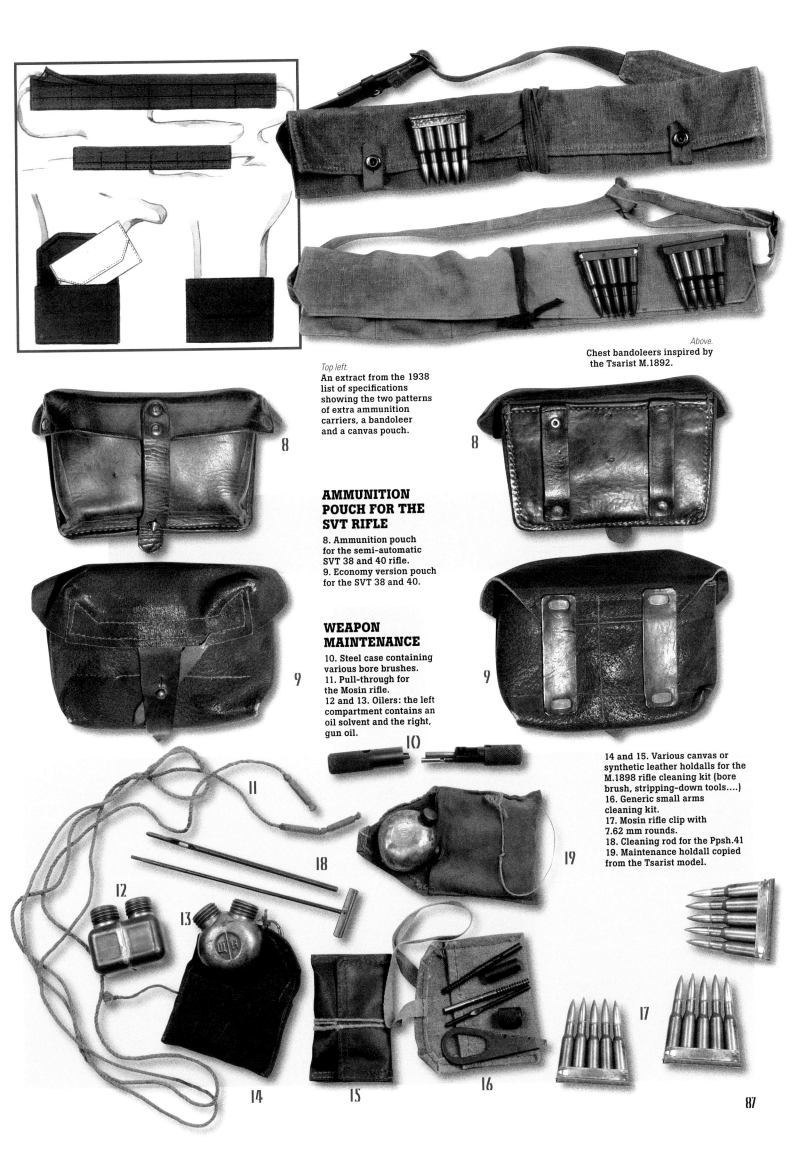

An extract from the 1938 list of specifications showing the two patterns of extra ammunition carriers, a bandoleer and a canvas pouch.

Above.
Chest bandoleers inspired by the Tsarist M.1892.

AMMUNITION POUCH FOR THE SVT RIFLE

8. Ammunition pouch for the semi-automatic SVT 38 and 40 rifle.
9. Economy version pouch for the SVT 38 and 40.

WEAPON MAINTENANCE

10. Steel case containing various bore brushes.
11. Pull-through for the Mosin rifle.
12 and 13. Oilers: the left compartment contains an oil solvent and the right, gun oil.

14 and 15. Various canvas or synthetic leather holdalls for the M.1898 rifle cleaning kit (bore brush, stripping-down tools….)
16. Generic small arms cleaning kit.
17. Mosin rifle clip with 7.62 mm rounds.
18. Cleaning rod for the Ppsh.41
19. Maintenance holdall copied from the Tsarist model.

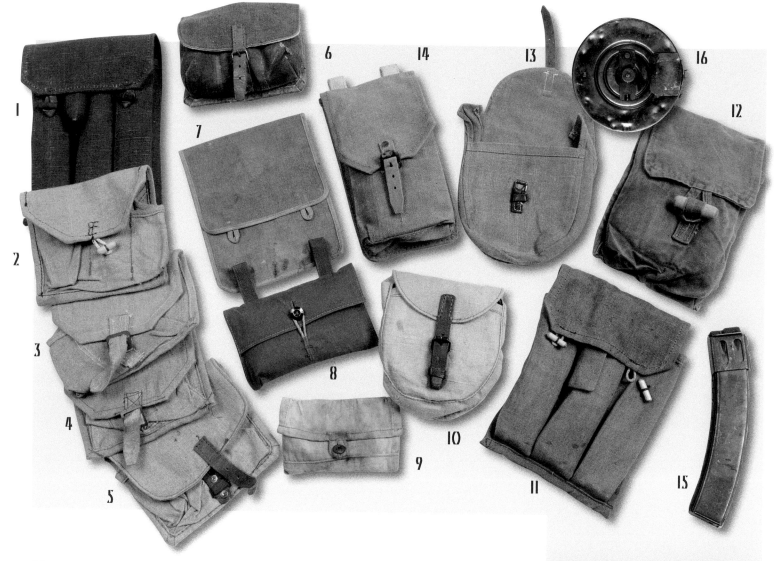

Magazine carriers, grenade pouches

The PPSH.41 submachinegun drum magazine was carried in a round canvas pouch closed with a leather strap. The PPS.43 straight magazine pouch had three compartments closed by wooden toggles.

The grenades were housed in a pouch with three compartments for the F-1 grenade, and two for the RGD-33 grenade.

MAGAZINE CARRIERS FOR SUBMACHINEGUNS, GRENADE POUCHES

1 and 11. Canvas magazine pouches for the Ppsh 41 and 43 SMG box magazines.
2 to 6. Various triple-compartment pouches for F1 grenades.
7. Canvas holdall for flying personnel, containing a survival kit (rations, matches....)
8 and 9. Canvas extra ammunition pouches.
10 and 13. Pouch for the 72-round drum Ppsh 41 magazine.
12 and 14. Canvas carriers for the RGD33 type grenades.
15. Curved 35-round box magazine for the Ppsh.41
16. Drum magazine for the Ppsh.41.

Below.
Illustration showing the grenade pouch worn across the shoulder.

The grenades commonly used by the Red Army: RTD.42, RGD.33, and its segmented sleeve to transform it into a fragmentation grenade, F.1. fragmentation grenade.

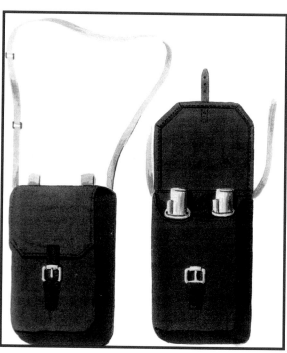

Pistol/revolver holsters

There were a great variety of holsters: the M.95 for the Nagant revolver, a leather or canvas and leather oblong-shaped holster for the Tokarev pistol with a magazine compartment, the M.03 made of leather or canvas and leather for the Korovine pistol, not forgetting the various canvas holsters for flare pistols. The lanyards were made of leather or webbing and leather.

1 to 4. Nagant revolver holsters.
5. Leather and canvas, and leather lanyards for revolvers and pistols.
6. Leather holster for the TT33 pistol.
7. and 8. Suspended leather holster for the TT33 pistol.

Left.
Flare pistol carrier. The bottom side-opening compartment holds a selection of flares.

Right.
An illustration showing the type RTD.42 (top) and F.1 (below) hand grenades.

Рис. 71. Ручная граната РГ-42: *a* — общий вид (без запала); *б* — вид в разрезе;
1 — корпус; *2* — фланец корпуса; *3* — деревянная пробка; *4* — лента;
5 — разрывной заряд; *6* — центральная трубка; *7* — запал УЗРГ

Above.
First type flare pistol.
(Michael Baskette collection)

Left.
Second type flare pistol.
(Mark Retzlaff collection)

Mess tins, cups and water bottles

There were three types of mess tin (*Kotelok*) in service with the Red Army.

★ The model 1924 was round and equipped with a handle.
★ The model 1926 was similar to the model 24, but higher.
★ The model 1936, which looked like the German model and which was equipped with a canvas cover.

Various types of mess tins. From the left, the M.26 round mess tins, M.36 German-style mess tins, enamelled plate, enamelled or aluminium drinking cup, regulation and hand made cutlery.

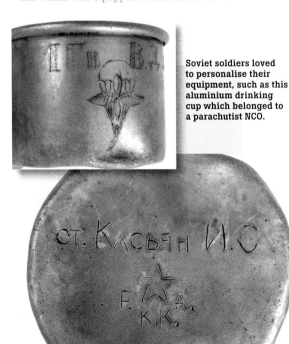

Soviet soldiers loved to personalise their equipment, such as this aluminium drinking cup which belonged to a parachutist NCO.

Right.
Marking on the handle of a 1940 dated M.36 mess tin.

Bottom.
The canvas mess tin cover.

Right.
Marking on the underneath of a 1940 dated M.26 mess tin.

Bottom right.
Marking on the lid of a 1938 dated M.36 mess tin.

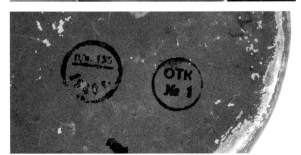

In their messes, the officers ate out of china cups and plates, bearing the Red Army (RKKA) markings.

Water bottles

Made of aluminium or glass, it held 0.75 litre. A cotton cover allowed it to be hung from the belt. The cover fitted with a long strap to allow it to be worn over the shoulder was reserved for medics.

Left.
Dessert and soup plates. The RKKA markings are clearly visible. Milk pot, USSR marked cutlery, regulation vodka glasses and traditional bread.

Left.
Markings on a 1942 dated water bottle cover.

Water bottles and their canvas covers. The model to the bottom left was worn over the shoulder and reserved for medics.

Glass water bottle in a 1938 type cover equipped with a strap and hook for the belt.

Left.
Markings on the bottom of a 1939 dated aluminium water bottle.

Glass and aluminium water bottles.

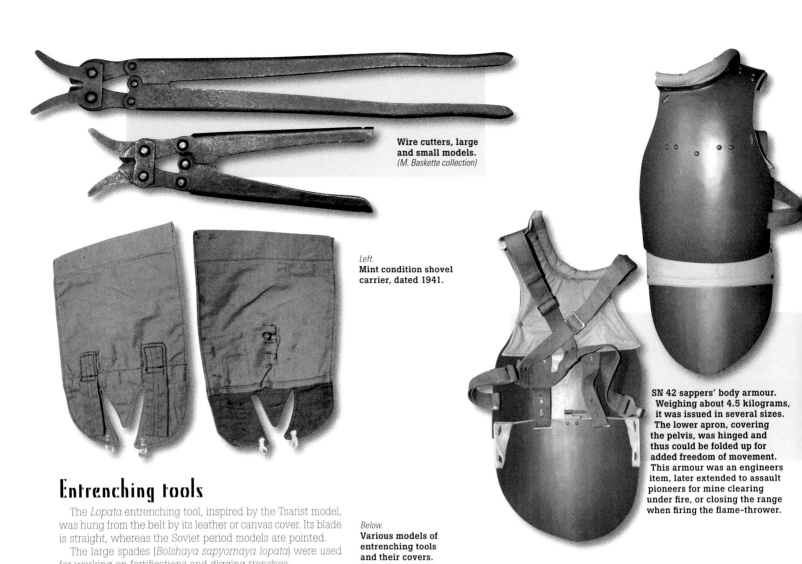

Wire cutters, large
and small models.
(M. Baskette collection)

Left.
Mint condition shovel
carrier, dated 1941.

SN 42 sappers' body armour.
Weighing about 4.5 kilograms,
it was issued in several sizes.
The lower apron, covering
the pelvis, was hinged and
thus could be folded up for
added freedom of movement.
This armour was an engineers
item, later extended to assault
pioneers for mine clearing
under fire, or closing the range
when firing the flame-thrower.

Entrenching tools

The *Lopata* entrenching tool, inspired by the Tsarist model,
was hung from the belt by its leather or canvas cover. Its blade
is straight, whereas the Soviet period models are pointed.

The large spades (*Bolshaya sapyornaya lopata*) were used
for working on fortifications and digging trenches.

Axes, cutters, picks and so on, were also issued.

Below.
**Various models of
entrenching tools
and their covers.
At top is a large
spade for platoons.**

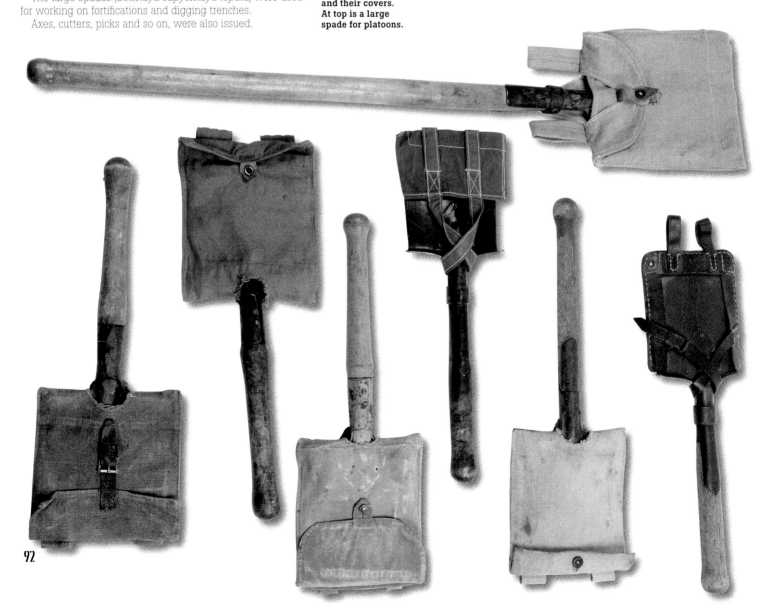

The *Plaschch-palatka* tent section/poncho (1.70 by 1.70 meter) was made of strong canvas and closed down the front with wooden toggles. One of the edges could be tightened with a string to fashion a hood. A slit on one side allowed for one arm to slide through.

Right.
Engineers satchel, slung across the shoulder and held by a waist strap. The main compartment holds mines and explosives, smaller pockets are for fuzes, detonating cord, etc. The short straps on the bottom are for holding a small bag of flags for marking cleared paths.

Entrenching tool markings. The spade at left bore Tsarist army markings, which were deleted by drilling out during the Soviet era.

The entrenching tools removed from their covers. At right, the hand axe and cover.

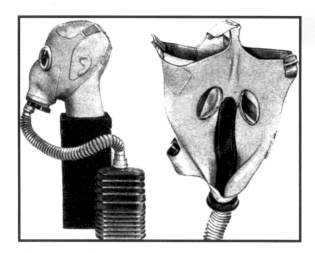

MOD-08 gas mask.

Sch M.1 model 1938 gas mask.

Below right.
Illustration showing the Sch M.1 and MOD-08 gas masks, as well as how to store them in the carrier.

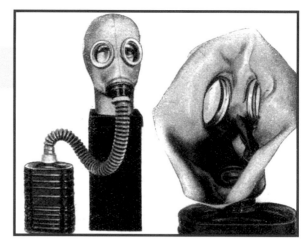

Gas masks

The service mask was held in a special canvas carrier with, or without, side compartments. Inside were placed the mask, ноэс, filter, cape and a protective hood, spare eye-pieces…

There were the following models: Sch M.1 (model 1938), MOD-08 (model 1937), GP-2 (variant of the Sch M1), BS-T5 (model 1929-35), BN-T5 (model 1930).

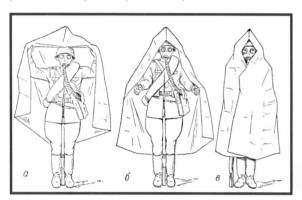

How to wear the antigas cape.

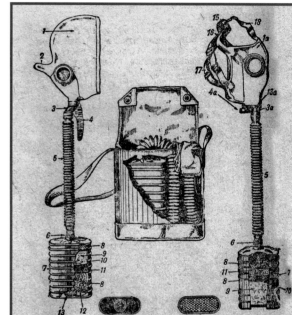

The impermeable rubber decontamination suit.

For decontamination, it was necessary to wear the *Obshe-voiskovoï zachitnyi komplek*t, a watertight rubber suit.

It should also be noted that horses were also equipped with a gas mask.

MOD-08 gas mask and its accessories: spare eye-pieces, various types of carriers, antigas cape and hood, antigas ointment.

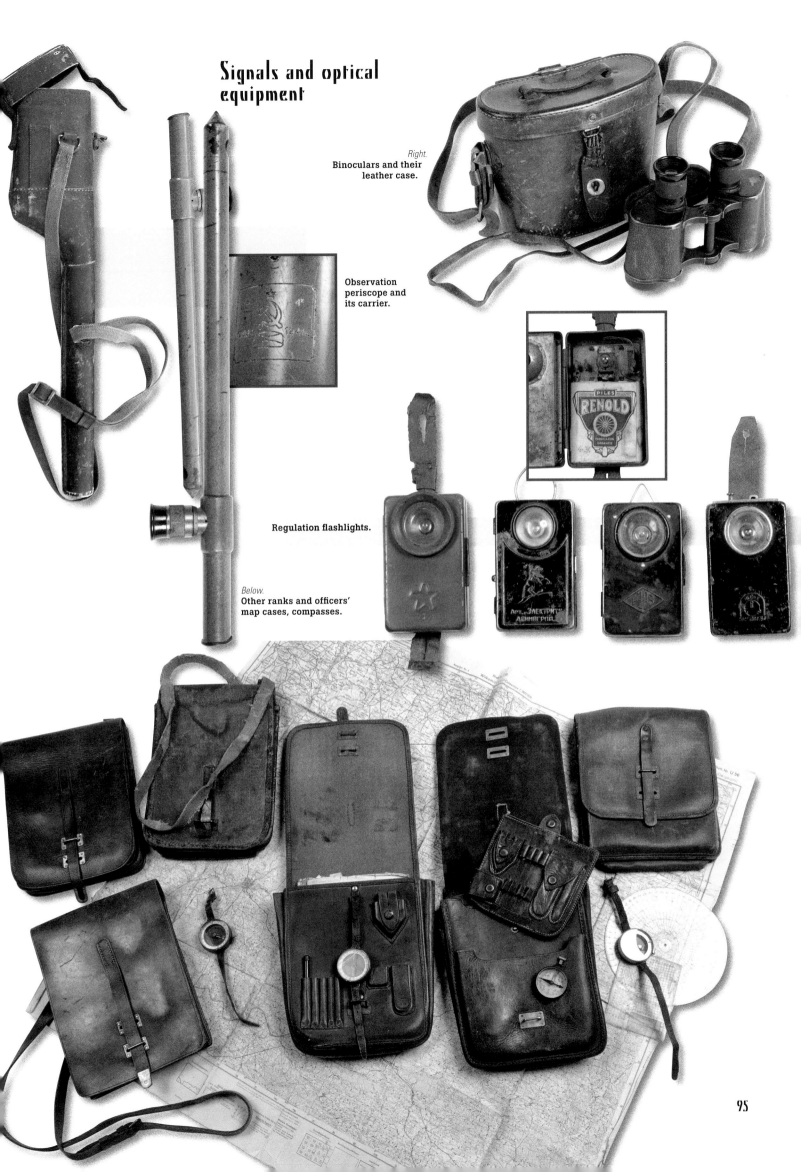

Signals and optical equipment

Right.
Binoculars and their leather case.

Observation periscope and its carrier.

Regulation flashlights.

Below.
Other ranks and officers' map cases, compasses.

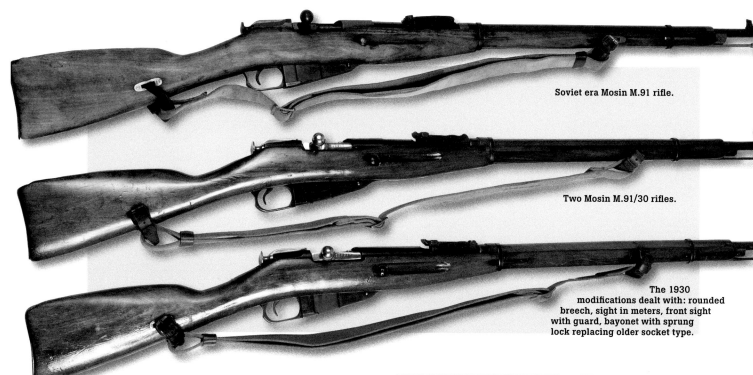

Soviet era Mosin M.91 rifle.

Two Mosin M.91/30 rifles.

The 1930 modifications dealt with: rounded breech, sight in meters, front sight with guard, bayonet with sprung lock replacing older socket type.

When war started, the great majority of Red Army weaponry was of old design. However, the period of 1938-40 had seen the introduction of new weapons, but these were not totally ready in 1941.

Soviet engineers had come up with new technology that allowed for mass production and savings in metal, but these revolutionary weapons were not quite yet perfected. Because of the initial setbacks, the removal of factories and a lack of raw materials, the Soviets were forced to improve their weapons by making them more efficient and easier to manufacture.

Right. Mosin M.91/30 rifle markings. Left, a rifle produced by the State arsenal at Tula in 1925; right, a weapon made in 1943.

Below Semi-automatic SVT.40 rifles.

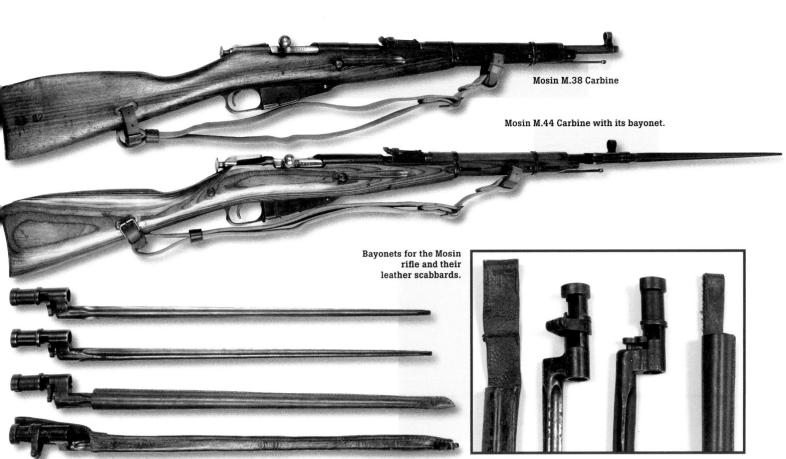

Mosin M.38 Carbine

Mosin M.44 Carbine with its bayonet.

Bayonets for the Mosin rifle and their leather scabbards.

After four years of trials, the SVT-36 rifle, then the 38, resulted in the SVT-40, the first mass produced semi-automatic rifle.

The Ppd 34/.38, then 40, sub machine-gun, lead to the Ppsh.41, then the Pps.43. These two weapons were remarkable in their simplicity and their high rate of fire.

Side arms were the Nagant M1895 revolver (seven 7.62 mm rounds) and the TT33 automatic pistol (eight 7.62 mm round magazine).

M.40 trench knife markings. They are generally marked ZIK (*Zavod Imienti Kirova*), the name of the factory where they were made, at Zlatoust. Remember that combat knives were not only reserved for parachute units, but more particularly to scouts and assault pioneers.

Year of manufacture markings on the receiver of a SVT.40 and on the stock.

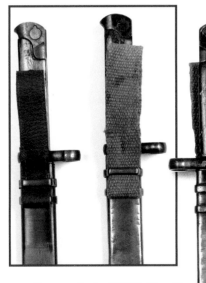

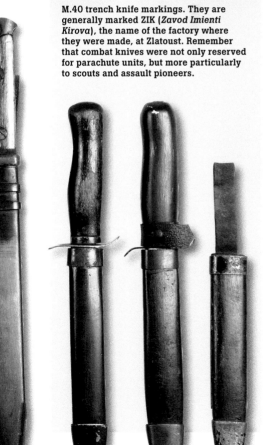

Bayonets for the SVT.40 rifle, with the leather or canvas frog.

Above.
**PPSH.41 with a curved box
and drum magazine.**

**Tokarev TT.33
automatic pistol.**
The TT (Tula, a State
arsenal, and Tokarev, its
designer) was a variant of the Browning
patent, with alterations to make it easier
to manufacture and maintain. It had an
8-round magazine of 7,62-mm ammunition,
a round similar to the Mauser C-96's, a
very popular handgun in Russia at the time.
The trigger was single action, without safety.
(Bertrand Gaskowiak collection)

PPS.43 with curved box magazine.

Right.
This colourised print
from 1945 shows a Frontovik
armed with the Pps43 SMG.
His M.43 Gymnastierka is
adorned with the Guards
badge. Also note the lend-
lease leather belt, with its
square open faced buckle.

The M.1895 revolver was a Belgian design by Messrs Nagant, who had also developed a new service rifle for the Czar's army. Rugged and efficient, it fired a rimmed 7.62-mm calibre round. Although superseded by the new TT33 pistol, the Nagant was still made and issued up until the end of WW2.
(Bertrand Gaskowiak collection)

The DP.28 light machine gun, designed by the engineer Degtyarov, was introduced in 1928. Sturdy and reliable, it was fed by a 47-round pan magazine. Its only defect was its bipod, which did not stand up to hard use. The DP.28 magazines were carried in special canvas bags or metal boxes (see also page 141).

INFANTRY WEAPONS

	calibre	weight	rounds	length	remarks
HANDGUNS					
Nagant M.95 Revolver	7.62		cylinder 7		
Tokarev M.33 Pistol	7.62		magazine 8		
RIFLES/CARBINES					
M.91/30 Mosin	7.62	3.9	5	1.23	can receive a
M.36 Simonov	7.62	4.3	10 or 15	1.23	telescopic sight
M.38 Tokarev	7.62	4	10	1.22	ditto
M.40 Tokarev	7.62	3.9	10	1.22	ditto
M.38 Mosin	7.62	3.5	5	1.03	
M.44 Mosin	7.62	3.5	5	1.02	folding bayonet
SUBMACHINE GUNS					
PPD M.38-40	7.62	3.5	71	0.785	weight unloaded
PPSH M.41	7.62	3.5	71	0.840	weight unloaded
PPS M.43	7.62	3	35	0.616	full auto only
LIGHT MACHINE GUNS					
M.28 Degtyarov	7.62	8.4	48	1.27	full auto only
MACHINE GUNS					
M.10 Maxim	7.62	55	250	1.10	weight with mount
M.38 Degtyarov	12.7	40	50	1.62	2-wheel mount
M.39 Degtyarov	7.62	25	250 & 500	1.17	tripod mount
M.43 Goriunov	7.62	40.5	250	1.17	2-wheel mount
ANTI-TANK RIFLES					
PDR M.41 Degtyarov	14.5	17.3	1	2.00	bipod
PTR M.41 Simonov	14.5	20.9	5	2.14	magazine-fed
PTR M.43 Simonov	14.5	20.3	5	2.14	

Side view of the M.36 helmet. The shape of the peak is characteristic, as is the small comb at the top.

MLADSHIY-SERZHANT, 8TH INF. DIV., 229TH REGIMENT MINSK, JUNE 1941

Above.
The M.35 collar tabs are raspberry coloured for the infantry.
The enamelled triangle corresponds to the rank of Mladshiy-Serzhant.
The infantry insignia of two crossed rifles on a target is not official.
Right. Detail of the Osoaviakhim badge for pre-military antigas and air raid defence.

This Mladshiy Serzhant wears the field uniform: M.36 helmet, M.29 Gymnastierka, M.35 breeches and M.38 boots. The equipment comprises of a M.36 haversack on which the mess tin and its cover are attached, as well as the tent section. The leather belt supports the water bottle, the entrenching tool in its leather cover, the bayonet and its leather scabbard, and the black leather ammunition pouches. The weapon is the Mosin 91/30 rifle.

MLADSHIY-SERZHANT, 8TH INF. DIV., 229TH REGIMENT MINSK, JUNE 1941

The haversack front straps hook onto the top of the ammunition pouches.

Below.
View of the M.36 haversack, with the mess tin and tent section. The entrenching tool and water bottle are suspended from the belt.

The other haversack front strap goes under the arm and attaches to the bottom of the pack.

Above.
The 1940 pattern infantry collar tabs now have a central red coloured stripe, with three enamelled brass triangles for rank.

Right.
The distinguished Red Army soldier badge was established on 14 November 1939.

Left.
The Vorochilov sharpshooter badge was created by the Osoaviakhim pre-military organisation in 1932.

Right and opposite page.
This Starchiy-Serzhant wears the new field uniform introduced in 1939. M.39 helmet with circular liner, M.35 Gymnastierka, M.35 other ranks' breeches and M.38 boots. The equipment comprises of a M.39 leather and canvas haversack with the rolled tent section. The leather belt supports the M.37 ammunition pouches, an extra green canvas ammunition pouch, M.41 bread bag, water bottle, entrenching tool with its canvas cover, the bayonet and its metal scabbard and canvas loop for the SVT.40, gas mask carrier and the enamelled drinking cup. The weapon is the semi-automatic SVT.40 rifle.

Left.
The water bottle and
the entrenching
tool with its canvas
cover. The enamelled
drinking cup was
held by the closing
tab of the gas
mask carrier.

Above.
Side view of
the helmet and
equipment.

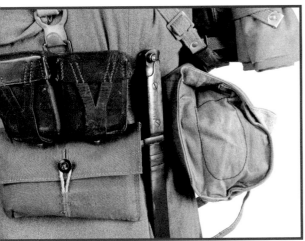

Left.
The extra rectangular
canvas ammunition pouch
is suspended from the belt.

Left.
The SVT.40 rifle bayonet
and the M.41 bread bag
are suspended on the
belt, on the right side.

KAPITAN, 42TH INF. DIV., 44TH REGIMENT. BREST-LITOVSK FORTRESS, JUNE 1941

Above.
View of the infantry piped officer's side cap.

Above and bottom.
Close up of the 1935 pattern collar tabs. The second view shows the screw back attachment of the enamelled rank rectangle and the arm insignia.

Right.
Close up of the rank stripe at the bottom of the sleeves.

Right.
This infantry officer wears the M.35 tunic known as the 'French.' The garment has 1935 pattern collar tabs and rank insignia at the bottom of the sleeves. The side cap and breeches have raspberry piping. The man wears ankle boots with 1938 pattern leather leggings. The uniform is completed by the officers' belt with star.

Left.
This pilot wears the blue M.35 blouse. Normally reserved for the walking out uniform, it was often used for every day wear to instil esprit de corps. The colours could vary as these uniforms were often tailor-made. The embroidered pilot's wings on the left sleeve are seen here in the classic configuration of the end of the nineteen-thirties. The flying helmet is an exact copy of the Luftwaffe's LKpW 101 (due to the collaboration between the two countries after the German-Soviet pact of 1939). The goggles are typical of the period and worn over the helmet. There are two bulbous ventilation slits over the lenses (these were no longer present on post-war models).
(J. Faure and J-F. Moret collection)

The Soviet Air Force

As with its tank arm, in 1941, the USSR had the largest quantity of combat aircraft, but most were obsolete. Furthermore, the invasion caught the Air Forces as they were undergoing a deep reshuffling. The Russians had realized that the squadron was too small a tactical unit, and its format was enlarged in order to form Air Divisions. These divisions were directly seconded to ground forces, but this doctrine only dispersed the available strength, a defect compounded by faulty communications. Losses in 1941 were staggering, with as many as 16,000 planes claimed by the Germans.

New reforms were enforced during the Spring of 1942, and the 1st Air Army was established with a centralised command. Air Forces units assigned to Fronts also had their own command. Fighter regiments now had a third squadron and flew a single type of aircraft.

If the Soviet Air Force had been found lacking in 1941, its influence was felt the following year. Personnel training and operational worth greatly improved. More and more modern planes were turned out by displaced factories, at a monthly rate of 2,000 machines. In January 1944, the Soviet Air Forces could boast 11,000 planes on the Eastern front and all through the war, the industry had turned out a total of 137,271 planes. The Allied effort also provided for 20,000 British and American combat planes.

A pilot captain ready for flight in the summer of 1941. The grey 1935 pattern tunic is accompanied by dark blue 1938 pattern breeches. The officers' boots are worn when weather permits. However, regulations forbade this practice in July 1941, for safety reasons: these boots complicated treatment in the event of injury. This pilot has the simplified PL3M harness. He also has a flying helmet equipped with radio wiring, standard goggles, gauntlet gloves and a 1940 pattern map case.
(J. Faure and J-F. Moret collection)

Left.
Junior-lieutenant with a blue M.35 tunic, worn with matching 1938 pattern breeches. The cap is the 1940 pattern which differs from the model 1937 by its sky blue band. The large maps will be placed inside the air forces 1940 pattern map case for the flight.
(J. Faure and J-F. Moret collection)

KAPITAN 124TH INF. DIV., 781ST REGIMENT. ROVNO, AUGUST 1941

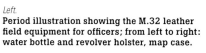

Left.
Period illustration showing the M.32 leather field equipment for officers; from left to right: water bottle and revolver holster, map case.

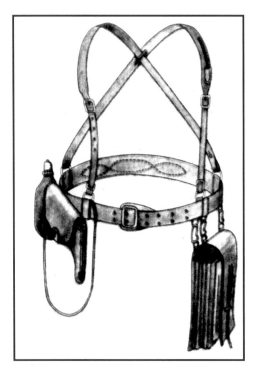

Above.
Detail of two pocket compasses.

Below.
On a military scale map: the removable compartment of a map case with several crayons and a bakelite pencil, a pocket compass, an officer's wristwatch and issue whistle.

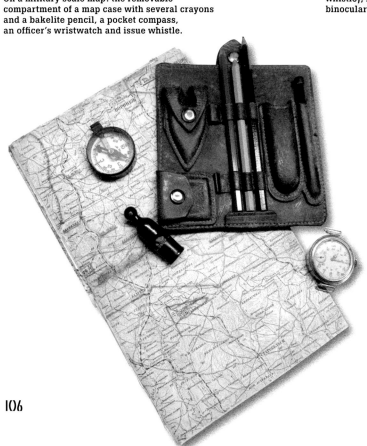

This infantry captain wears the M.35 Gymnastierka with the M.35 collar tabs. He wears a side cap with raspberry piping for the infantry. The blue breeches are the 1935 pattern for officers, worn with soft leather officers' boots. Equipment is as follows: M.32 belt, suspension straps (one supporting the whistle), revolver holster, binoculars and map case.

Top.
Cavalry officer portrait. The collar insignia can be clearly seen.

Right.
This cavalry officer wears the M.27 Budionovka in the colours of his arm, M.35 Gymnastierka with M.35 collar tabs and sleeve rank insignia, blue breeches, boots and spurs. The belt, Nagant revolver holster, cross straps, map case and sabre hanger are all model 1932.

Above.
Close up of the M.35 collar tab.

Left.
Close up of the rank chevrons.

(Continued on page 108)

Left.
This cavalryman is equipped with
a leather sabre hanger.

Above.
A regulation form for the description of a
squadron's horses. It contains information on
the horse, as well as the horseshoe numbers,
the special gas mask, name of cavalryman etc.

Below.
The saddle and its harness.

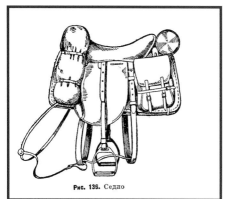

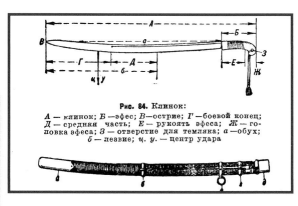

Above.
An extract from the cavalry regulations showing
the shape and size of the sabre.

Below.
Another extract showing how to hold the sabre.

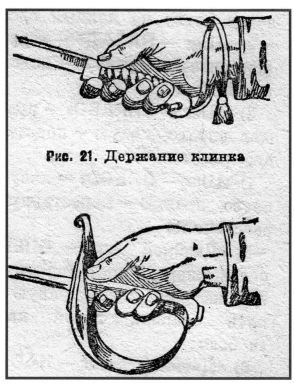

Extract from cavalry
regulations showing
the cavalryman with
all his equipment. Note
the wearing of the cap.

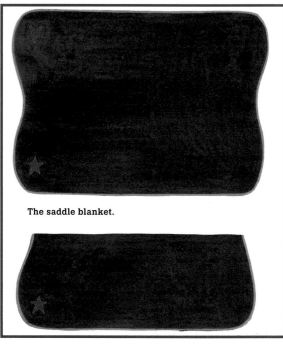

The saddle blanket.

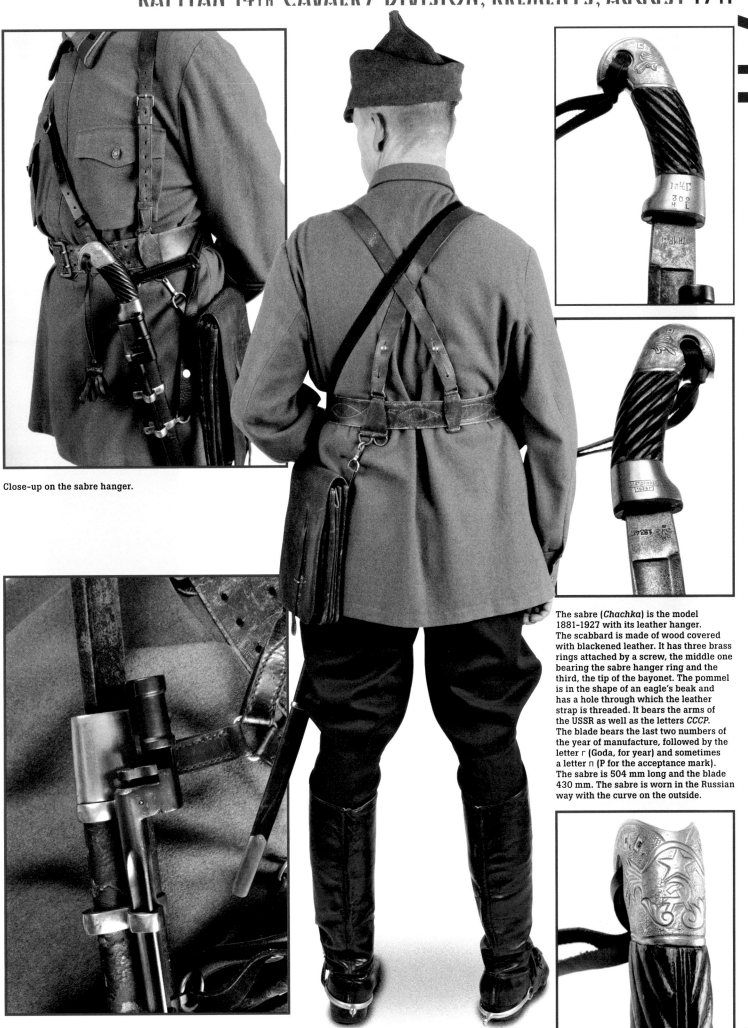

Close-up on the sabre hanger.

The sabre (*Chachka*) is the model 1881-1927 with its leather hanger. The scabbard is made of wood covered with blackened leather. It has three brass rings attached by a screw, the middle one bearing the sabre hanger ring and the third, the tip of the bayonet. The pommel is in the shape of an eagle's beak and has a hole through which the leather strap is threaded. It bears the arms of the USSR as well as the letters *CCCP*. The blade bears the last two numbers of the year of manufacture, followed by the letter г (Goda, for year) and sometimes a letter п (P for the acceptance mark). The sabre is 504 mm long and the blade 430 mm. The sabre is worn in the Russian way with the curve on the outside.

Left and below.
Close up of the M.35 collar tabs and the underside of the collar, cut from a piece of dark blue cloth, identical to the breeches'.

This artillery officer wears the 1935 pattern cap and tunic. The latter has collar tabs and rank insignia at the bottom of the sleeves. The leather officer equipment is the model 1932. The breeches are blue with red artillery piping. The boots are the officers' model in soft leather.

This engineers transmitter carries a shovel in its canvas cover. The M.35 tunic has 1935 pattern collar tabs for this service branch (black background, blue piping). He is equipped with a M.38 haversack, ammunition pouches, water bottle, gas mask in its bag. The steel helmet is still the model 1936. Being a member of the technical troops, he is armed with a Mosin M.38 carbine, more practical due to its shorter length.

Left.
Close up of the 1940 pattern collar tab.

This despatch rider wears the M.40 helmet. The M.35 tunic has collar tabs with a black background and red piping for the artillery with the transportation units metal device. The protective goggles are one of the numerous variants in service. The equipment consists of a belt, leather ammunition pouch, a breast ammunition pouch copied from the model 1892 containing thirty rounds and a NCO map case. The gloves are made from leather. This motorcyclist is armed with the Mosin M.38 carbine.

This young officer wears an open collar version of the "French" tunic that appeared in 1925. The breast badge is the model 1936 for excellent artilleryman. The collar tabs are those of the artillery (black background, golden piping for officers) with the arm insignia (two crossed cannon). The breeches are blue with red piping. He wears high boots.

MLADSHIY POLITRUK - 129th INF. DIV., 343rd REGIMENT SMOLENSK, AUGUST 1941

Left.
Close up of a collar tab.

This Mladshiy Politruk prepares to exhort the troops to resist the invader. Political commissars wear a red star at the bottom of each sleeve, with an embroidered wire hammer and sickle in their centre. These stars were deleted in August 1941, but they continued to be worn up to 1942-43. The collar tabs are the other ranks' model, but bear officers' rank insignia. The M.35 tunic has piping in the colour of the arm, this being raspberry here for the infantry. The Order of the Red Star, introduced in 1930, is pinned over the left pocket.

Above.
Close up of the sleeve star.

Left and below.
Staff officers of an artillery unit in 1942. At the top left hand side are two political commissars. The enlargement allows us to see the sleeve star, collar tabs and newly introduced wound stripes.

116

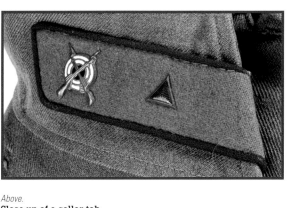

Above.
Close up of a collar tab.

Right.
An illustration showing how to use the mosquito net issued to NKVD troops.

This border guard is ready to set off on patrol accompanied by his dog. The cap has the distinctive green crown, black band and raspberry piping. The border guards colours are also visible on the 1935 pattern tunic's collar tabs: green background with raspberry piping. The tunic also bears the Voroshilov marksman badge and the antigas instructor insignia. The breeches are blue without piping for NCOs. The man is equipped with an ammunition pouch, the Mosin rifle bayonet in its leather scabbard and a flashlight. The use of dogs was very common in the Red Army, mostly within border guards units for tracking, and by the engineers for mine-clearing operations and anti-tank combat.

Below.
A Border guards dog handler team on the Leningrad front in 1941.

SERZHANT - 17TH NKVD BRIGADE, 206TH BATTALION
KHARKOV, JULY 1941

Above.
Close up of a collar tab.

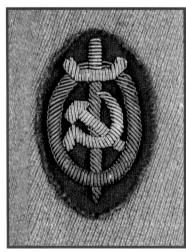

Right.
**Close up of the NKVD
troops sleeve insignia.**

This NCO belongs to the armed branch of the State Security (NKVD).
Their embroidered insignia is sewn onto the sleeves of his
Gymnastierka. The collar tabs and cap piping are in NKVD colours: brick red and raspberry.
The rank insignia are those of junior army officers, but they are not equivalent.
The man is equipped with a FED camera made under licence from
Leica. These cameras bear the NKVD initials on top of the case.

Below.
M.35 peaked cap in the NKVD distinctive colours.

Left.
Close up of the beret.

Below.
**View of the false breast pocket
and the Order of the Red Star.**

**Close up of the collar tabs and the way that the medical
services and rank insignia are attached.**

Above.
Cuff piping.

This medical officer wears the M.41 uniform: beret and dress
with integral belt and fold down collar. The collar tabs
are in medical services colours: green background,
red piping. The insignia is gold coloured.
The Order of the Red Star, introduced in
1930, is pinned over the left pocket.

Below.
**The female officer in the centre
wears the M.41 uniform.**

Tank troops were issued with a grey coloured uniform, introduced by order 176 of 3 December 1935. The specific collar tabs have a black background with gold piping, the tank insignia is gold coloured. The breeches here are blue with red piping, but they also existed in grey cloth.

Left.
The crash helmet seen here is the canvas model, with double lens goggles specific to tank units (see below).

Right.
Close up of the sleeve rank insignia.

Left.
Portrait of a tank major, Hero of the Soviet Union. The collar tabs, as well as the decorations, are clearly visible.

Left
The model 1941 side cap, a cloth star is sewn behind the enamelled star.

This officer, a veteran of the battle of Lake Khasan, wears a M.35 tunic, modified by order 251 of 1 August 1941: the buttons, collar tabs and rank insignia are all drab green. The breeches here are the officers' model, blue with piping. The equipment is made of leather. The only decoration is the commemorative insignia for the battle of Lake Khasan of 6 August 1938 against the Japanese.

Left.
Commemorative insignia for the battle of Lake Khasan

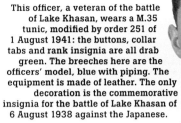

Above.
Close up of the collar tab and rank insignia, modified following order 251 of 1 August 1941.

Above.
Close up of the green buttons, also modified by order 251 of 1 August 1941.

The Nagant service revolver and its holster (see also on page 89 and 99)

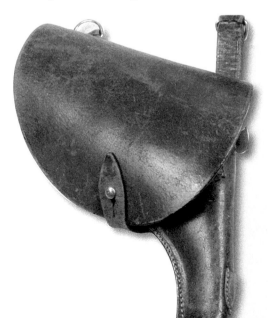

FIGHTER PILOT LEITENANT, SEPTEMBER 1941

Left
A 1940 dated variant of the leather coat. The junior lieutenant collar tabs are those originally sewn on, as are the simplified version pilot's wings for the field uniform.
(J. Faure and J-F. Moret collection)

The leather coat was regulation wear in the air forces since the nineteen-twenties. Most of the time it is black, but some brown coloured coats were also issued. The dog hair boots, introduced in 1940, protect well against the cold. The soles are made of sewn felt. The gloves, also introduced on this date, leave the fingers free, but have a movable section that allows the wearer to transform them into mittens. This system ensured better protection against the cold when dexterity was not necessary. The uniform is completed by a 1940 pattern leather flying helmet. Equipment is reduced to the minimum: belt, suspended holster for the Nagant revolver and map case.
(J. Faure and J-F. Moret collection)

Left
Period photograph of a pilot. He wears the fur-lined 1940 pattern flying suit and dog hair boots. The flying helmet with wide fur-lined collar is also the 1940 pattern. The goggles are copied from the German model.

Above.
Pilot lieutenant in a flying suit. The leather coat is worn with the 1940 pattern flying helmet, lined with sheep or yak skin. This pilot wears unlined gauntlet gloves, stipulated like most of the flying equipment, in 1940. The goggles are exact copies of the Luftwaffe model (*Fliegerschutzbrille*). The parachute harness is a PL3M, a simpler and more comfortable version. This parachute was used throughout the war by the Soviet air forces.
(J. Faure and J-F. Moret collection)

Below.
A group of pilots. All of the greatcoats have the embroidered wings.

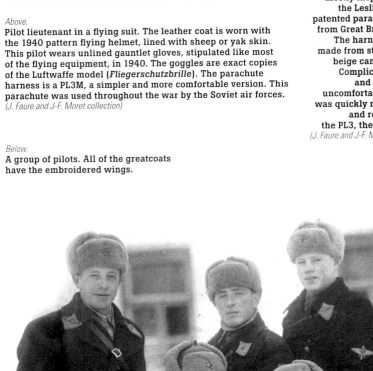

This captain has just landed unscathed after bailing out. He wears the grey cloth 1935 pattern Gymnastierka. This very rare garment appeared in 1941. He has gathered up his PL1 parachute canopy, mostly inspired by the Leslie Irvin patented parachutes from Great Britain. The harness is made from strong beige canvas. Complicated and very uncomfortable, it was quickly modified and replaced by the PL3, then the PL3M.
(J. Faure and J-F. Moret collection)

KRASNOARMIEYETS - 331st INF. DIV., 1116th REGIMENT MOSCOW, DECEMBER 1941

Right.
During this first winter of the war, the new padded garments have not yet been issued to all Red Army personnel. This infantryman wears, therefore, the M.35 greatcoat, recognisable by its collar tabs and pointed sleeve cuffs. The winter headwear is the Budionovka.

Above.
The soldier now wears a wool balaclava along with the steel helmet. The infantry collar patches are raspberry red with black piping. The enamelled device is not regulation.

Above.
Rear view of the greatcoat collar and its construction.

Below.
Rear view of the greatcoat with its back belt.

The inside of the greatcoat and its markings.

This scout wears the white snow suit originally designed for ski battalions during the conflict with Finland. This cotton garment is very loose fitting. It is closed by nine large buttons and has a fairly large hood so that it can be worn with the helmet. The gloves are integral, and drawstrings allow the garment to be better adjusted. Common practice within scout units, the PPSH.41 sub machine-gun has been camouflaged with a strip of white fabric.

Below.
The Valenki winter felt boots.

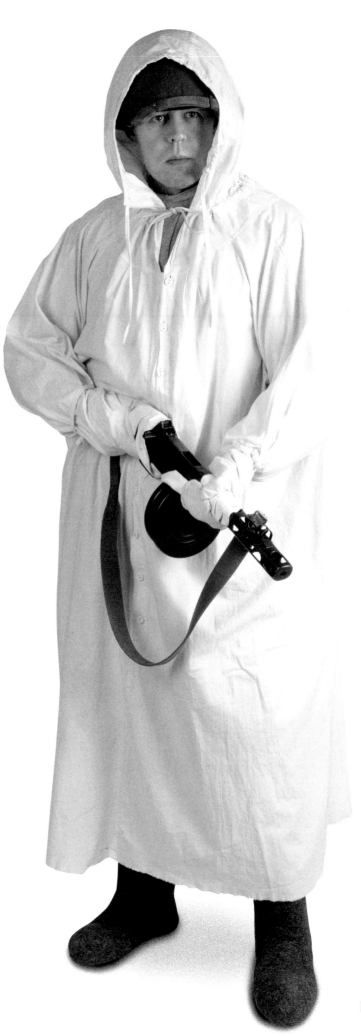

SERZHANT - 46TH TANK BRIGADE, 1ST BATTALION VOLKOV, JANUARY 1942

The leather uniform gave good protection against the cold and the fires that could break out inside a tank. The short model was reserved for other ranks and up to the rank of lieutenant. The long model was reserved for officers from the rank of Kapitan. The leather trousers have canvas cuffs to make it easier to wear with boots. It has two pockets, a fob pocket, and a short tightening strap at the back. The equipment comprises of a belt with a suspended holster for the side-arm. The helmet is padded for the winter.

Below left.
Close up of the collar tabs.

Below.
This photo shows us the early leather uniform in service within the Red Army.

Left
Tank crew Mladshiy Serzhant with a M.35 tunic. Note the shape of the cap. The print is captioned *"Stalingrad-1941. A souvenir of our time at the tank and armour school."*

Above.
A nice portrait of a tank Starchina. The helmet is made of leather and the jacket canvas. Note the goggles with side lenses.

View of the false pocket and buttons.

Above.
This armoured unit radio operator wears blouse collar tabs with a black background and red piping, but with the signals arm insignia. He wears the padded Tielogreïka jacket and the canvas helmet.

Below.
Detail of the fleece-lined winter padded helmet for AFV crews.

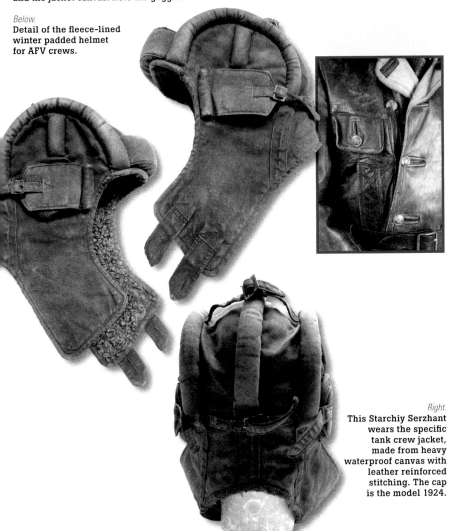

Right.
This Starchiy Serzhant wears the specific tank crew jacket, made from heavy waterproof canvas with leather reinforced stitching. The cap is the model 1924.

Above.
These three pilots wear dashing Irvin Pattern 1942 flying jackets with breast stitching.

This leitenant's flying suit is worn underneath a British-made Irvin flying jacket supplied as part of the Lend-Lease agreement along with Hurricane and Spitfire fighters. These jackets were much liked and became the object of a veritable trade, especially in units that were mostly issued with them, such as the French Normandie-Niemen squadron.

(J. Faure and J-F. Moret collection)

Left.
A group of pilots in Germany. The Irvin jacket is obviously very popular.

Close up of the subdued 1941 green collar tab.

A the end of the winter of 1941-42, this subaltern wears the officers' model greatcoat with collar tabs, as stipulated by decree 253 of 1 August 1941. The M.24 field cap is made of khaki canvas and has an enamelled star. The belt is the 1935 pattern and supports a leather holster for the Nagant revolver.

Left.
Rear of the greatcoat with its back belt.

FIGHTER SQUADRON KAPITAN, AUGUST 1942

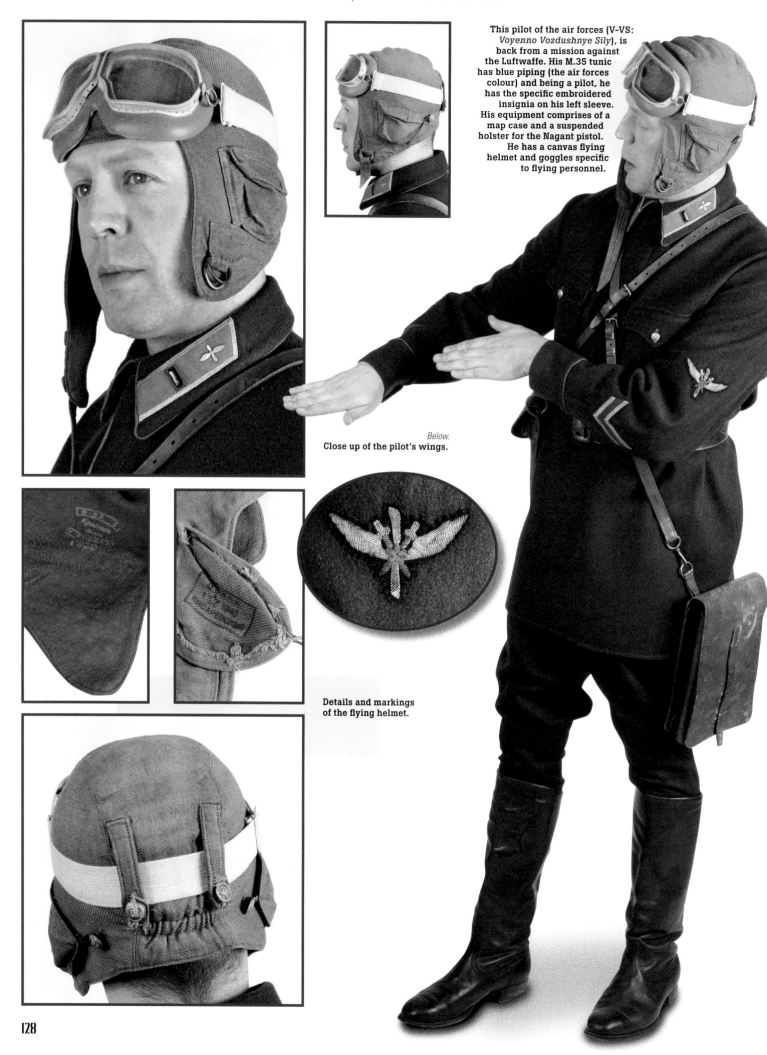

This pilot of the air forces (V-VS: *Voyenno Vozdushnye Sily*), is back from a mission against the Luftwaffe. His M.35 tunic has blue piping (the air forces colour) and being a pilot, he has the specific embroidered insignia on his left sleeve. His equipment comprises of a map case and a suspended holster for the Nagant pistol. He has a canvas flying helmet and goggles specific to flying personnel.

Below.
Close up of the pilot's wings.

Details and markings of the flying helmet.

KRASNOARMEYETS OF THE 5TH PENAL BATTALION, AUGUST 1942

This soldier wears the tunic issued only to disciplinary units. It is made of thick canvas and is closed by five buttons. This punished soldier is not allowed to wear a red star on his side cap. The only equipment is a belt, ammunition pouch and a Mosin 91/30 rifle.

Above.
Markings inside the tunic.

Detail of the rifle ammunition pouches.

TANK CREW 189TH TANK BRIGADE, 135TH BATTALION. STALINGRAD, AUGUST 1942

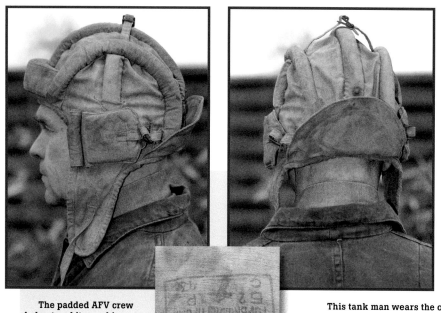

The padded AFV crew helmet and its markings.

This tank man wears the overalls only issued to armoured and motorised unit personnel. These are worn over the uniform. They have a breast pocket, two thigh pockets and are closed by five metal buttons. The overalls can be in blue, grey or sand coloured fabric, as seen here in this picture. The belt is made of leather and canvas, and a map is placed in the thigh pocket. The helmet is made of grey canvas and has a pair of goggles. The unused earphones rest around the neck.

THE URAL TANK MEN SONG
written by Grigoriy Slavine in 1942.

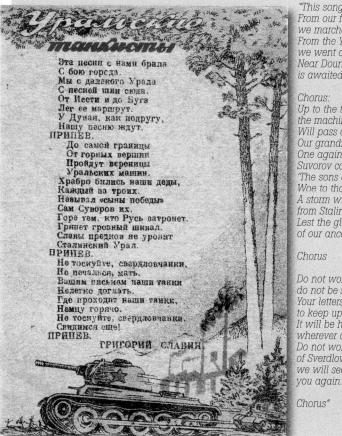

"This song helped us capture towns
From our faraway Urals
we marched with this song.
From the Yesta to the Bug
we went on our way.
Near Dounay, our song
is awaited like a girl.

Chorus:
Up to the top of the mountains
the machines of the Urals
Will pass one after the other
Our grandfathers bravely fought
One against three.
Suvorov called them
'The sons of Victory"
Woe to those who attack Russia
A storm will blow
from Stalin's Urals
Lest the glory
of our ancestors be tarnished

Chorus

Do not worry, girls of Sverdlovsk,
do not be sad, Mother
Your letters find it hard
to keep up with our tanks
It will be hot for the Germans
wherever our tanks pass
Do not worry,   girls
of Sverdlovsk,
we will see
you again.

Chorus"

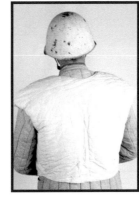

Left.
Close up of the Shapka-Ushanka under the helmet.

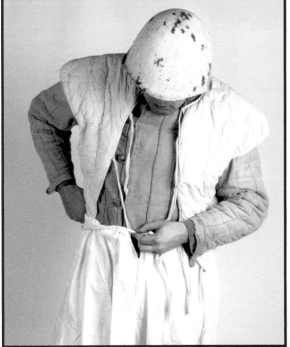

The white snow smock has now been replaced by a suit comprising of a jacket and trousers. A sleeveless padded coat is worn underneath to protect against the cold. The garment is similar in design to the smock. It is made of cotton and is very roomy, with adjustment drawstrings, a large hood and integral gloves. Veterans have reported that this type of garment was very fragile and had to be replaced after three or four patrols.

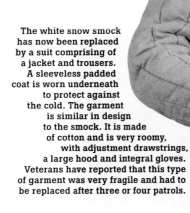

Putting on the white snow suit and camouflaging the weapon, a PPSH.41 with box magazine.

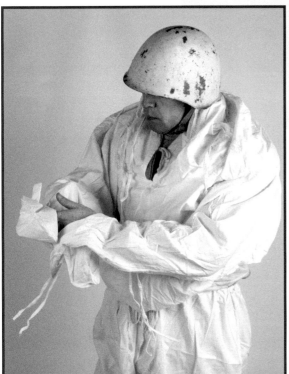

KRASNOARMEYETS OF THE 29TH INF. DIV., 128TH REGIMENT. STALINGRAD, FEBRUARY 1943

This scene allows us to see the winter uniform, comprising of the following garments: Shapka, padded *Tielogreïka* jacket, padded *Vatnie-sharovari* breeches and *Valenki* boots made of compressed felt for the second soldier. The infantryman on the left is armed with the SVT.40 rifle, his equipment calls for a leather ammunition pouch, bayonet, leather belt and entrenching tool. The Frontovik on the right is armed with the formidable PPSH.41, his canvas and leather belt supports a canvas magazine pouch.

1943

Our two soldiers eat at a table made from a German ammunition box, with an American ration crate being used as a seat.

Hülsenkart.
12,2 cm K.390/1(r)u./2(r)

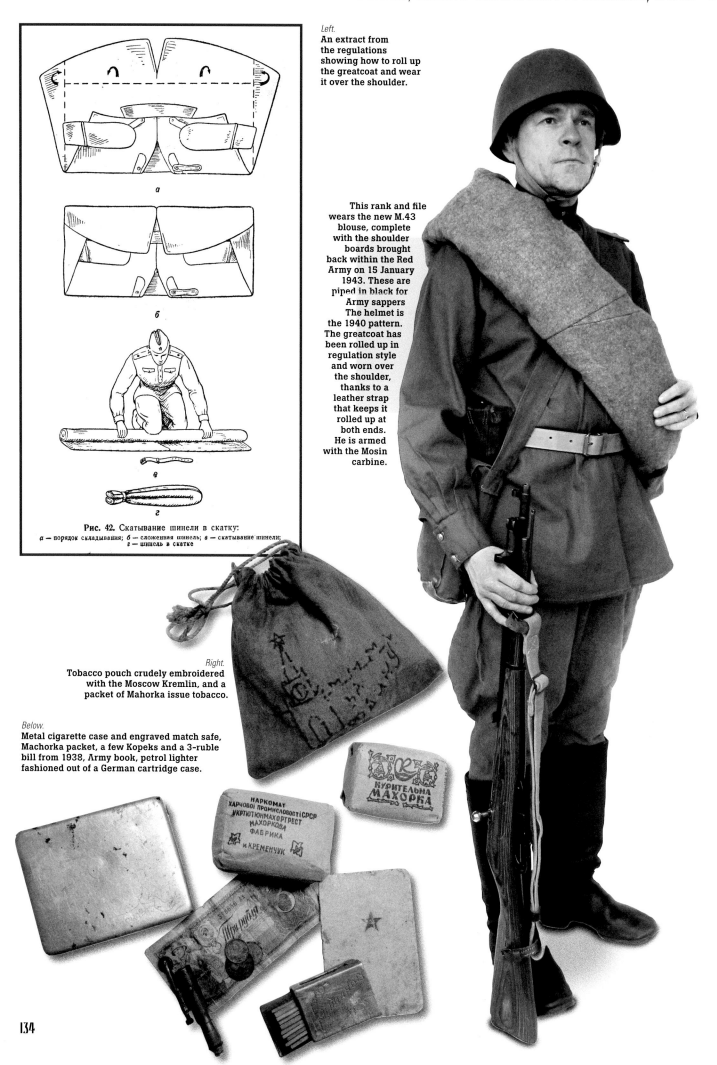

Left.
An extract from the regulations showing how to roll up the greatcoat and wear it over the shoulder.

Рис. 42. Скатывание шинели в скатку:
а — порядок складывания; *б* — сложенная шинель; *в* — скатывание шинели; *г* — шинель в скатке

This rank and file wears the new M.43 blouse, complete with the shoulder boards brought back within the Red Army on 15 January 1943. These are piped in black for Army sappers The helmet is the 1940 pattern. The greatcoat has been rolled up in regulation style and worn over the shoulder, thanks to a leather strap that keeps it rolled up at both ends. He is armed with the Mosin carbine.

Right.
Tobacco pouch crudely embroidered with the Moscow Kremlin, and a packet of Mahorka issue tobacco.

Below.
Metal cigarette case and engraved match safe, Machorka packet, a few Kopeks and a 3-ruble bill from 1938, Army book, petrol lighter fashioned out of a German cartridge case.

Left.
This infantry major wears
the M.32 field equipment.
The shoulder boards are highly visible.

As the new 1943 tunics have not
yet been issued, our Major has
modified his 1935 tunic.
The fold-down collar has been transformed
into a straight collar, false breast pockets
and the new shoulder boards have been
added. The cuff piping has been retained.
He wears the Order of the Red Banner
in its suspended version with
ribbon. He has a padded
Finka officer's fur hat.
The breeches are the officers'
model, the model 1932
leather equipment is worn.

Close up of the false breast
pockets, as well as the
Order of the Red Banner.
(Author's photos)

135

SNIPER OF THE 90TH GUARDS INFANTRY DIVISION, 272ND REGIMENT BIELGOROD, AUGUST 1943

The camouflage suit with "amoeba" type patches, seen here in its summer version, was generalised at the beginning of the war. This particular suit, in brand new condition, retains very bright colours. The Soviets formed several sniper divisions throughout the war. This sniper is equipped with a SVT.40 and a model PU scope.

THE TEN BEST RED ARMY SNIPERS

Name	Unit	Number of kills
MI Surkov	4th Inf. Div.	702
VS Kvachantiradze	259th Inf. Regt.	534
IM Sidorenko	122nd Inf. Regt.	500
NY Ilyin	50th Guards Inf. Regt.	494
IN Kulbertinov	23rd ski brigade and 7th Para. Regt.	487
VN Pchelintsev	11th Infantry Brigade	456
MI Budenkov	59th Guards Inf. Regt.	437
FM Ohlopkov	1243, 234, 259th Inf. Regt.	429
FT Dyachenko	187th Inf. Regt.	425
VI Golosov	81st Guards Inf. Regt.	423
SV Petrenko	59th Guards Inf. Regt.	422

Above and left.
Close up of the shoulder board and cuff piping.

This officer wears a M.43 tunic which differs from the other ranks' pattern by the two breast pockets and the piping on the cuffs. Note the Guards Badge, as well as the medals for Bravery in combat and that for the Defence of Moscow. The cap is the 1935 pattern in infantry colours: green top, raspberry red band and piping. Our lieutenant is equipped with a leather belt, a Tokarev pistol in its holster and a PPS.43 submachinegun.
(Author's photo)

Detail of the medals for Bravery in combat and for the Defence of Moscow; and the Guards badge.

KRASNOARMEYETS OF THE 23rd INF. DIV., 89th REGIMENT ZHITOMIR, JUNE 1944

This infantryman, armed with the Mosin 91/30 rifle, wears the new model 1943 tunic, recognisable by its standing collar and its shoulder boards. He wears the M.40 helmet. His equipment comprises of:
– the tent section rolled up and worn over the shoulder, the ends of which are placed inside the mess tin
– leather and canvas belt and ammunition pouches. The high boots have been replaced by ankle boots and puttees.

Left.
These two Frontoviks wear the pocket-less tunic which is now issued to all personnel. The boots and belt are made of leather.

Right.
The NCO on the left wears the M.43 tunic with pockets, the field cap, and has a campaign medal. The man on the right wears the M.43 tunic without pockets, upon which is pinned an Excellent Soldier badge.

Side view of the equipment. The ends of the tent section are placed inside the old model mess tin. The water bottle is made of glass. The carrier suspended from the belt at left is for the RGD stick grenades (close up below).

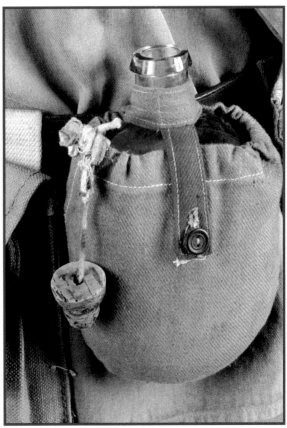

PULJEMJOTSCHIK OF THE 42nd INF. DIV., 459th REGIMENT MOGHILEV, JUNE 1944

Our light machine gunner wears the new M.43 uniform. The medals for the Defence of Stalingrad and Combat Merit are worn on the left side. His equipment comprises of a canvas and leather belt, grenade carrier, gas mask bag, entrenching tool and water bottle. He carries the Myeshok soft backpack.

Right.
Rear view of the equipment and how to attach the mess tin to the top of the backpack. The bag is closed at the top by knotting the straps together.

Note.
Nuradilov Hanpasha was acknowledged as being the Red Army's most excellent light machine gunner, with an official tally of 920 enemy killed and seven machine-guns destroyed.

Below.
Detail of the grenade pouch.

Two-man LMG team consisting of a gunner and his No 2. The latter carries the special bag for the LMG drum magazines.

Below.
The magazine carrier for the DP.28 LMG and the metal case for three magazines. These cases could be placed in the special carrier.

Another typical silhouette of the late-war Red Army soldier: side cap, M.43 other ranks' tunic (no chest pockets) with field uniform shoulder boards, cotton breeches and leather boots. He carries a long model, three compartment magazine pouch for the SMG. The PPS 43 was a lighter weapon than its illustrious predecessor of 1941. It was also faster and less expensive to manufacture.

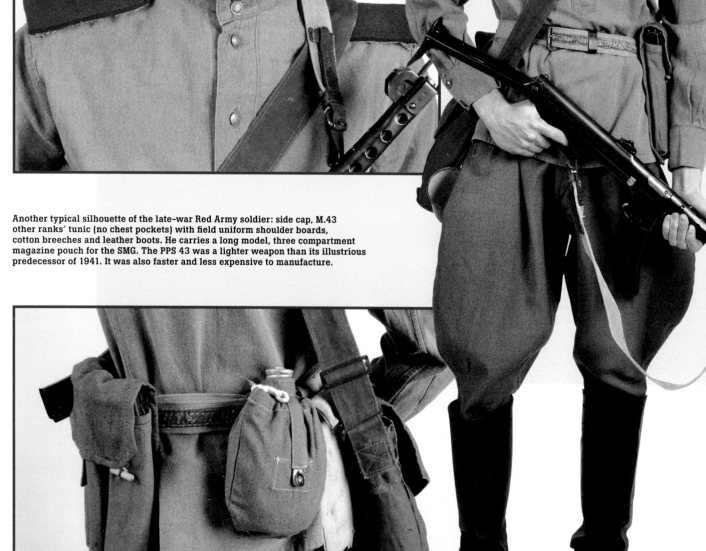

SERZHANT OF THE 37TH GUARDS INFANTRY DIVISION, 114TH REGIMENT SLONIM, JULY 1944

This Hero of the Soviet Union proudly wears his gold star on his M.43 tunic, pinned above all the other orders and medals: Order of Lenin and the medal for the Defence of Leningrad. On the right are the Order of the Red Banner, Order of the Great Patriotic War 1st class, and below, the Excellent mine engineer badge and Guards Badge. The M.43 tunic with pockets has rigid shoulder boards. The two prong belt, although reserved for officers, was very popular with NCOs.

Above.
**On this shot, our Hero wears the officers'
M.35 belt with cut-out star.**

Below.
Portrait of Captain Skvortsov, a Hero of the Soviet Union.

Left.
Close up of the integral gloves.

This scout (*Razvedchik*) wears the summer pattern camouflage clothing, with tufts of artificial grass attached on the jacket and trousers. This suit is almost identical in its design to the "amoeba" model, but does not have a veil and has integral gloves.

As the garment is quite roomy, the equipment is worn underneath. The weapon is the PPS.43.

SERZHANT SANITARNY OF THE 71st GUARDS DIVISION, 74th MEDICAL BATTALION, AUGUST 1944

This medical orderly wears the 1943 uniform for female personnel. Indeed, the tunic has reversed buttoning and pleats on the chest. The skirt is the model 38. According to the veterans' accounts, the red cross arm band was very rarely worn. The water bottle is placed in a holder with a long strap used by medics. The bag contains, bandages, disinfectant etc.

Left.
Another view of the medical orderly, wearing the M.40 steel helmet as she gets closer to the front-line.

Left and below left.
Close ups of the shoulder board with the gold coloured medical services insignia, and the Excellent Medical Services Soldier badge. The buttons on this tunic are made of aluminium, note also the breast pleats.

Below.
A male medic wearing the red cross arm band. The pocket flashlight is attached to a greatcoat button, and he wears the soft assault pack.

Left.
These female soldiers have just been decorated with the Victory over Japan medal. They all wear the M.43 tunic with reversed buttoning, beret and skirt.

Left.
Extracts from the regulations concerning the use of the field dressing.

Below.
Various medic bags, light equipment bag, bandages, arm band and medical kit.

VOENNIY JURIST, HEADQUARTERS OF THE 259th PENAL COMPANY
SEPTEMBER 1944

Left.
The narrower shoulder boards are typical of medical, veterinary and military justice personnel.

This colonel on an inspection visit wears the new M.43 dress for female personnel: it features an integral belt, a stand and fall collar and shoulder boards. The beret remains the regulation headwear.

This scout, getting ready to go on patrol, wears the 'amoeba' camouflage scheme smock. This is the summer-autumn version with a more subdued green colour. His canvas blouse (also shown on page 66) bears the medal for Bravery in combat, the Guards badge, the Excellent mortar man badge (see page 19), and two wound stripes (one severe and one light wound). He is armed with a PPSH.41.

Above.
The hood is large enough to cover the helmet.

Below.
Close up of the thin and fragile face veil, which has been repaired.

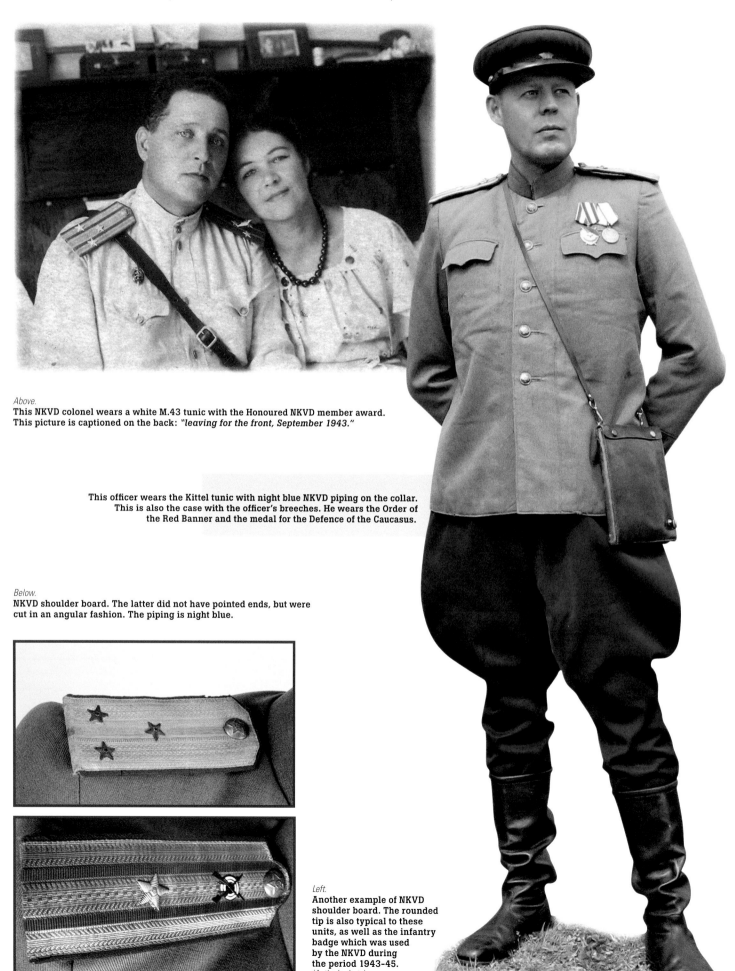

Above.
This NKVD colonel wears a white M.43 tunic with the Honoured NKVD member award. This picture is captioned on the back: *"leaving for the front, September 1943."*

This officer wears the Kittel tunic with night blue NKVD piping on the collar. This is also the case with the officer's breeches. He wears the Order of the Red Banner and the medal for the Defence of the Caucasus.

Below.
NKVD shoulder board. The latter did not have pointed ends, but were cut in an angular fashion. The piping is night blue.

Left.
Another example of NKVD shoulder board. The rounded tip is also typical to these units, as well as the infantry badge which was used by the NKVD during the period 1943-45.
(Author's photo)

Left.
An armoured corps Major with the Kittel tunic.

Left.
With this uniform, the shoulder boards are made of gold braid with red piping and bear the small gilded tank of the armoured corps.

This Major in service uniform wears the Kittel tunic. It has a five brass button closure and two breast pockets. The officer has been awarded the Order of the Great Patriotic War 1st and 2nd class, and the Guards badge. The medal for the Defence of the Caucasus is worn on the left side.

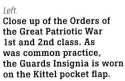

Left.
Close up of the Orders of the Great Patriotic War 1st and 2nd class. As was common practice, the Guards Insignia is worn on the Kittel pocket flap.

TANK MAN OF THE 1462ND ASSAULT GUN REGIMENT ROMANIA, SEPTEMBER 1944

Above.
Markings inside the overalls.

Above.
On this souvenir picture, the man on the left wears the blue overalls.

This tank man wears the blue overalls with integral belt, typical of armoured and motorised units. It is worn here over the M.43 tunic and breeches.

Right.
Another group of tank men. The three men wearing tank helmets also have the blue overalls. Among the others, we can make out two patterns of tunic, the side cap and peaked cap.

With the beginning of autumn, our man has been issued with a greatcoat. Of American Lend-Lease manufacture, it differs from Soviet made examples by the double row of buttons (instead of hooks) and by the wider back belt. The buttons are marked *Rex New Rochelle NY*.

Above.
These three tank crew men wear a thick pullover under the tunic, its collar is visible.

Below.
The shoulder boards are made more rigid by an internal piece of plastic.

RAZVEDCHIK OF THE 59TH GUARDS INFANTRY DIVISION, 183RD REGIMENT DEBRECEN, OCTOBER 1944

As a member of a Guards unit, our scout has been issued with the new camouflage outfit introduced in 1943. The camouflage scheme consists of small white leaves on a grey-green background. The two-piece outfit does not have integral gloves, but retains the veil, as well as the hood which is large enough to cover the helmet. He is armed with the PPSH 41 with curved magazine.
(Author's photo)

For the cold season, our officer wears the heavy, but warm, M.43 greatcoat. His head is covered with the Papasha, whose wear was extended to colonels of all arms and services as of 1943. The crown is green with an embroidered cross in the centre. He wears M.40 officers' boots.

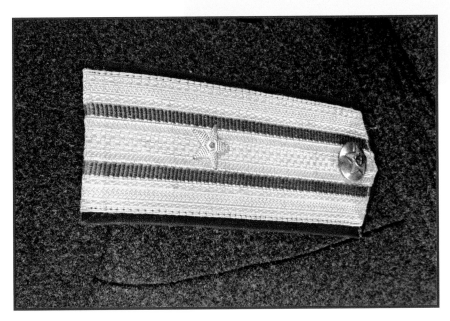

MEDICAL OFFICER, 71st GUARDS INF. DIV., 74th MEDICAL BATTALION BALTIC, DECEMBER 1944

This medical officer wears the double-breasted grey greatcoat with two rows of buttons and medical services shoulder boards for the service uniform. The shoulder boards have a silver background for non-combatant units. The cap has the distinctive brown-green top, dark green band and red piping.

To protect themselves from rain when in the field, officers have a canvas cape with a large hood. There are two slits for the arms.

MLADSHIY SERZHANT OF THE 14th GUARDS INFANTRY DIVISION, 33rd ARTILLERY REGT.-BRESLAU, FEBRUARY 1945

Left.
This portrait of a tank crew Krasnoarmeyets allows us to see the placing of badges and medals on the tunic. The Order of the Red Star is above the Excellent Driver badge and that of 'Guards' units. On the right is the medal for the Defence of Moscow, with a laminated ribbon. A closer look reveals that the shoulder boards are a mismatched pair and that the armoured corps insignia are badly attached. Note also the beard, a rare occurrence in the Red Army.

Below.
Close up of the artillery senior corporal's field uniform shoulder board.

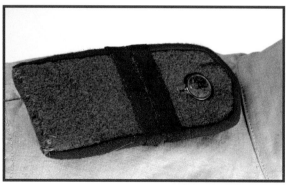

This veteran of the defence of Sebastopol, as indicated by the decoration pinned near the Medal for Bravery on the left, wears the model 1943 Gymnastierka without pockets.

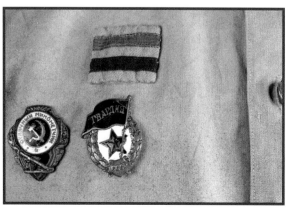

Left.
Two wound stripes are sewn on the right hand side. This experienced soldier has also been awarded with the Excellent mortarman badge, pinned next to the Guards badge.

This subaltern wears the warm and
fitted Polushubok coat. Made of reversed
sheepskin, it is closed by brass buttons.
The fleece is visible at the base of the sleeves.
As stipulated by the 1943 regulations,
the shoulder boards are present. The Shapka
is the officers' model with a painted tin star.
The mittens are made of grey canvas, The officer
wears the leather M.32 field equipment.

MLADSHIY SERZHANT OF THE 380th INF. DIV., 1264th REGIMENT GDYNIA, FEBRUARY 1945

Food rations are issued by an NCO. His M.43 tunic is the version with pockets, and his side cap is made of wool. He wears the medal for the Defence of Stalingrad.

Below.
Close up of the shoulder board with quartermasters insignia. The rank stripes here are made of gilded metal.

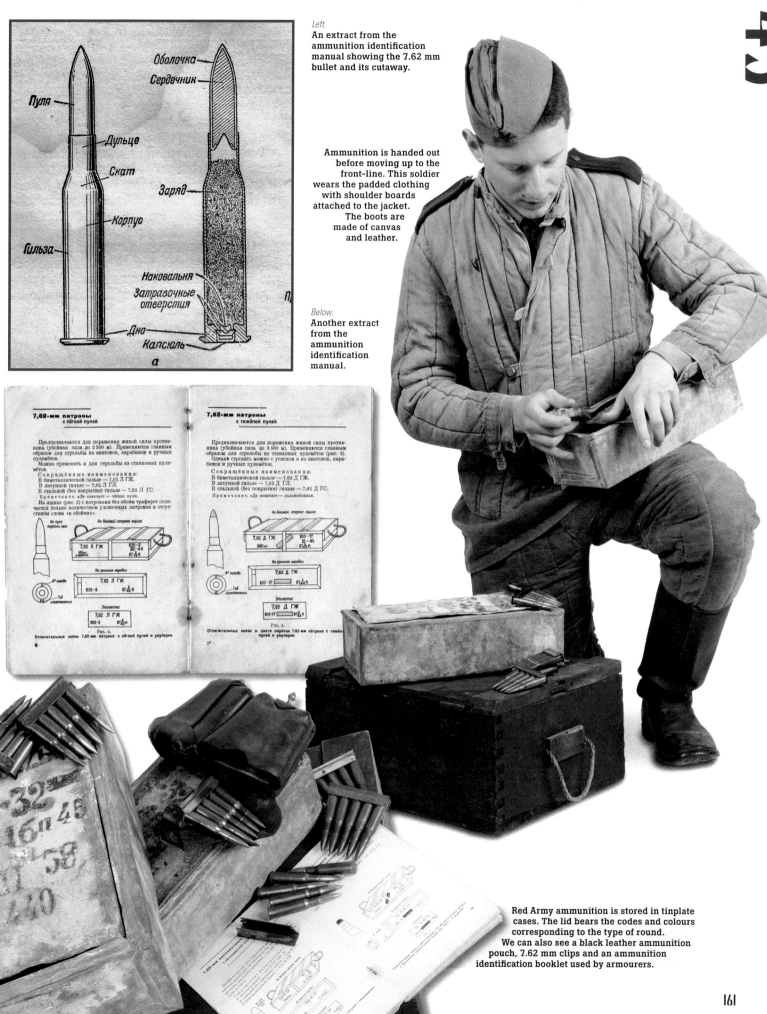

Left.
An extract from the ammunition identification manual showing the 7.62 mm bullet and its cutaway.

Ammunition is handed out before moving up to the front-line. This soldier wears the padded clothing with shoulder boards attached to the jacket. The boots are made of canvas and leather.

Below.
Another extract from the ammunition identification manual.

Red Army ammunition is stored in tinplate cases. The lid bears the codes and colours corresponding to the type of round. We can also see a black leather ammunition pouch, 7.62 mm clips and an ammunition identification booklet used by armourers.

KRASNOARMEYETS OF THE 312th INF. DIV., 1079th REGIMENT BERLIN, APRIL 1945

Above.
Reloading the carbine using a clip.

This Frontovik is fighting in the suburbs of Berlin. What a long journey it has been since the terrible summer of 1941! The outline of this Soviet infantryman is characteristic of the beginning of 1945: M.40 helmet, M.43 greatcoat, breeches, ankle boots and puttees. The equipment comprises of a leather and canvas belt, leather ammunition pouches and a bandoleer. He is armed with the Mosin M.44 carbine, with its folding bayonet.

Below.
Close up of one of the greatcoat's shoulder boards.

Wartime manufacture leather and webbing belt, dated 1944.

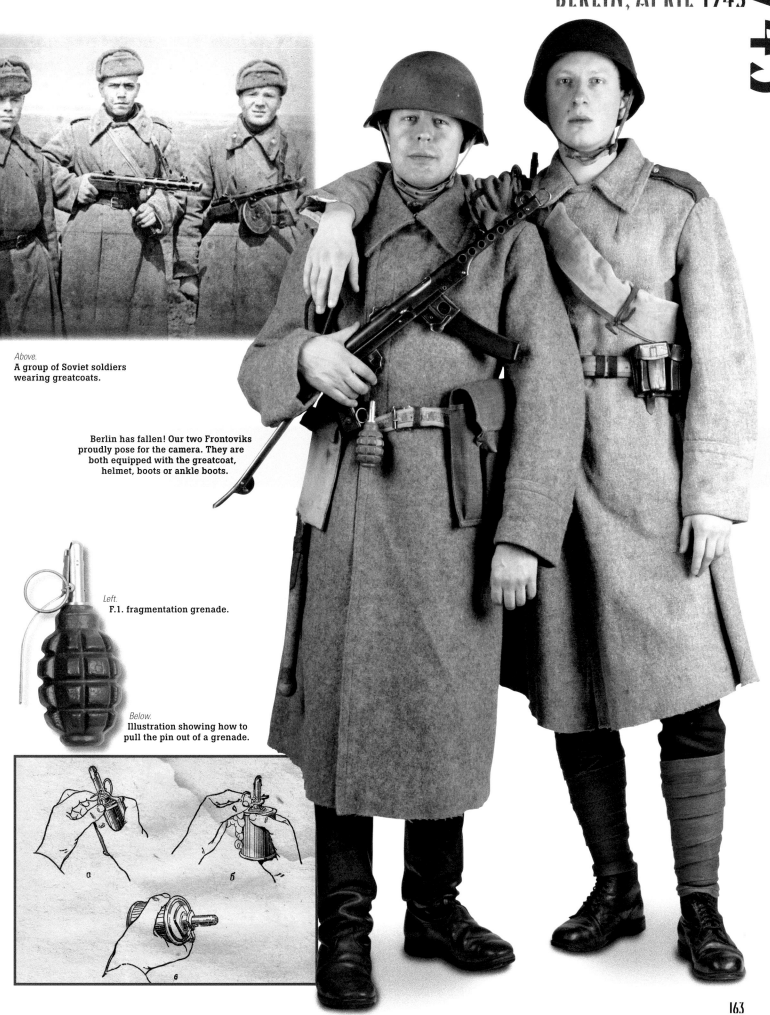

Above.
A group of Soviet soldiers wearing greatcoats.

Berlin has fallen! Our two Frontoviks proudly pose for the camera. They are both equipped with the greatcoat, helmet, boots or ankle boots.

Left.
F.1. fragmentation grenade.

Below.
Illustration showing how to pull the pin out of a grenade.

LEITENANT OF THE 38TH BORDER GUARDS REGIMENT, GERMANY-MAY 1945

Above.
M.1935 cap for the Border Guards, in green and red.

This officer's woollen tunic is representative of NKVD troops as it has two visible breast pockets, the angular ended shoulder boards are the dress uniform model. The officer has the medal for Combat Merit.

Between 18 to 27 August 1945, parachutists were in action against the Japanese in Manchuria. This man has been issued with the new camouflage suit with the saw-tooth camouflage scheme. The pattern is similar in design to the model 1943, but the leaves are made up of a multitude of small squares. This suit existed in an 'autumn' version with the addition of brown patches, and a 'summer' version with a yellowish background as seen here.

The equipment is now worn over the suit: a canvas and leather belt, RGD grenade pouch, water bottle, magazine pouch for the PPS43 and M.40 combat knife.

The field cap is made of canvas.

Above and bottom.
Photos of Soviet soldiers taken in Manchuria in 1945.

POLKOVNIK OF THE 48TH INFANTRY DIVISION, 22ND REGIMENT, MOSCOW-JUNE 1945

24 June 1945, time for the Victory parade in Moscow! For the event, this Colonel wears the Mundir dress tunic. Made from green cloth, it calls for collar patches and arm-of-service piping. In the case of a senior officer, the collar patches bear two stripes, and two cuff patches are sewn on the cuffs, in gold wire for the combat arms. The back of the garment features two false skirt pocket patches. The officer has been awarded with the following orders: two orders of the Red Banner, and Great Patriotic War 2d Class. His medals are: combat merit, defence of Moscow, liberation of Prague, victory over Germany and two Czech medals.

THE MOSCOW VICTORY PARADE, JUNE 1945

"The participants were chose in the following manner. Towards mid-May 1945, each division was ordered to designate five soldiers to represent it. If the unit commander deemed there were no worthy candidates, then no one was sent.

Lieutenant Pavel Paramovith Sabada was the only soldier standing for the 32d Guards Division. During the war, he had commanded the scout platoon of the 82d Regiment and could boast he had not lost a single man. He had won the Order of Alexander Newski, two orders of the Red flag, the order of the Red star and the medal for Bravery.

The chosen ones were despatched to Moscow at the Tcherniche-viskaya, Alexandreskaya, Octobriski and Lefortovoski barracks, and formed into ten regiments.

Parade rehearsals were held everyday on the runways at Frounze Airport, then the men would visit the tailor to try on the special uniform.

After the parade, Sabada gave his Mundir tunic to this brother, who altered it as a civilian jacket as he had lost everything in the war."

Testimony of Maria Sergeïnovna Sabada, Mladhiy-Leitenant with the 32d Guards Division, and spouse of Leitenant Pavel Paramonovitch Sabada.

Below.
Lieutenant Pavel Paramonovitch Sabada, flag bearer for the 1st Baltic front, during the Moscow Victory Parade on 24 June 1945 (see also page 175)
(Mrs. Sabada collection)

Left.
Mundir parade tunic for a Marines general, with distinctive red piping and shoulder boards. Embroidery is of gold bullion and buttons are the general officers' pattern. This general has won the orders of Lenin, Alexander Newski, Great Patriotic war and Red star; and the medals for 20th anniversary of the Red army, combat merit and for the defence of Sebastopol.

This colonel with the technical troops is identified by the silver wire patches on collar and cuffs. His decorations are the orders of the Red Banner and Great Patriotic War 2d class, medals for victory over Germany, liberation of Prague and for victory of Labour.

Below.
Flag pole finials and a portrait of Stalin in painted metal.

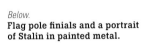

Above.
'At the Scout school, July 1942.' Note the sandals.

1945. Studio
portrait of two tankers.

Below.
1945, the staff of a motorized anti-tank unit. A wide array of uniform types is visible: field and service dress, shapkas, fur hats,
Kittels and blouses, officer's capes and leather coats, and even a German tunic for the soldier at top right!

Above.
1944. A group of scouts, the third soldier from left has the M.40 fighting knife.

Right.
1945. A very fine study of an Artillery Starchiy Serzhant posing with a Ppsh.41 SMG. His Shapka-Uchanka is brand new. The blouse collar was modified in Kittel-style. This NCO has been awarded with the Order of Glory, two medals for bravery and the medal for victory over Germany. Also note at left the Guards badge, and two excellent soldier badges (sharpshooter and artilleryman).

Below.
1945. Cavalryman Bachenko Ivan Petrovitch.

Above.
'1945, souvenir of the liberation of Zaporoje.'

1944. This Air Forces pilot has won the medal for merit.

Right.
These two Frontoviks pose with their Ppsh.41 SMGs.

1945. This NCO has won two orders of the Great Patriotic War, the Guards badge and the medal for the defence of Stalingrad.

Below.
1945. The guard is lined up for relief.

GENERALISSIMO J. V. STALIN

Left.
A late war official portrait
of Marshal Stalin

Above.
*'1945, liberation of Orekhov
from the Fascist aggressors.'*
Only one of the rankers has been
issued with the M.43 blouse.
The others have the older M.35
pattern with added shoulder boards.

Left.
Early war photo showing the
Budionovka worn with the greatcoat.

A flag from the 1st music school,
accompanied by a pair of infantry
Leitenant shoulder boards.
The latter bear the lyre insignia
specific to these units.

Below.
A musical group accompanied
by its dancers.

Left.
Portrait of a fighter pilot.
The colour of his uniform
shows that he belongs
to the naval air arm.

Below.
1944. NCO in field uniform.
An officer's belt is worn
for this souvenir picture.

The war is over. Photo taken in Germany, 1945. Many trophies
are visible. Back row, left to right: the fist soldier has a German
belt and Hitlerjugend knife, fifth soldier with a dagger, sixth
and seventh with German belts, the latter with a P.08 pistol.

May 7, 1945 in Berlin. These aviators pose in front
of the Brandenburg gate. The female officer has
various high decorations: the Great patriotic war,
Alexander Newski, Suvorov, Red flag and Honour
orders, Guards badge and Medal for bravery.

INDEX

VETERANS

Without the welcome and help of veterans, many a question would have remained unanswered. Therefore, I would like to thank them for opening their doors and their memories:

Lieutenant Kravchenko Vladislav Nikolaievitch. Commander of the 1st penal platoon of the 57th Army at Stalingrad, 199th Infantry Division. Veteran of the battle of Stalingrad, wounded twice. Kravchenko was awarded the Order of the Red Star and the Medal for Bravery.

Above.
Kravchenko Vladislav Nikolaievitch and his wife. The latter took part in the Moscow Victory parade on 6 August 1945. During this parade, she caught a glimpse of Marshal Stalin.

Right.
Starchiy-Leitenant Riabtchenko Mikhail Danilovitch, 399th, 206th, 149th and 61st Infantry Divisions. Veteran of the battles of Stalingrad, Kursk and Berlin. Four wounds, order of Alexander Newsky, two orders of the Red Banner and order of the Great Patriotic war.

Also, Starchiy Voyenfeldcher Lukas Helena Constantinova, Field Hospital 3261 and all the veterans who wished to remain anonymous.

ACKNOWLEDGEMENTS

I would also like to thank:
– My great friend Victor, his wife Olga, and their children Nicolas and Marie for their welcome, kindness and availability during my visits, not forgetting Vitali, his rugged car and unforgettable sauna
– Bertrand for sharing his vast knowledge of Soviet Union orders, medals and insignia
– Christophe and Larissa Guillemet for their invaluable translations!
– Fabrice Guillerm for looking through the text. Frédéric Coune, the photographer.
And also: Irène Rio, Céline Douet, Guilhem Touratier, Andrew Mollo, Christophe Civel, Daniel Blanchard, Jérôme Faure, Jean-François Moret, Michael Baskette, Mark Retzlaff, Bruno Renoult and Philippe Esvelin.
And lest we forget Bagi the dog.

Starschiy Voyenfeldcher Gaïdoukova Paulina Vassilievna, 142nd Marines Brigade. Battle of Sebastopol and Ravensbruck concentration camp

Leitenant Sabada Maria Sergeïnovna, 32nd Guards Division. Awarded the Orders of the Red Star and of the Great Patriotic War. Her husband, Leitenant Sabada Pavel Paramonovitch, 32nd Guards Division (died 10 April 1981) won the Order of Alexander Nevsky, two Orders of the Red Banner, the Order of the Great Patriotic War 1st and 2nd class, and the Medal for Bravery (see also page 166).

Below.
Issakova Olga Nicolaievna and her section commander, winner of the medal for the Defence of Stalingrad.

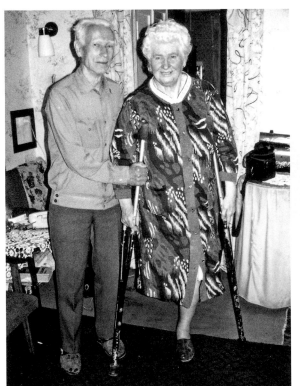

Above.
Issakova Olga Nicolaievna, 1028th Signals Regiment.

Constantin Sergueïvitch Sasa, partisan with the Pojaski Brigade, 90th Guards Division, and Antonina Yakovlievna Figlovskaya, Zhukov detachment 1942 (died in 2004).

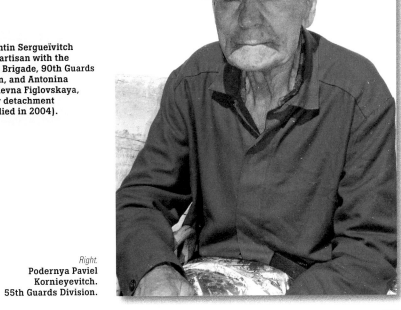

Right.
Podernya Paviel Kornieyevitch. 55th Guards Division.

CONTACT

Seeing as it is not possible to master a subject, I would like to make myself available to readers for any question, information or remarks. Do not hesitate to contact me at: riophilippe@orange.fr

Many articles by the author have been published in the French monthly *Militaria Magazine*, available by subscription and from: www.militaria-mag.com

BIBLIOGRAPHY

– Tietoja N-L: *n Armeijasta. 1941*
– *Taschenbuch russisches Heer, 15 April 1943*
– *New notes on the Red Army. 2-Uniforms and insignia. 1944*
– *Mémento sur l'armée soviétique* (French Army pamphlet May 1954)
– *Notes sur l'armée russe* (French Army pamphlet, June 1948)
– *Handbook on USSR Military forces. November 1945*
– *Identification handbook Soviet military weapons and equipment*
– *Soviet Order of battle. Vol. 1 to 13.* Charles C. Sharp
– *The Red Army order of battle in the Great patriotic war,* Robert G. Poirier and Albert Z. Conner. Presidio Press
– *Type et uniformes de l'armée rouge vus à Berlin en 1945.* Editions du Panache 1946
– *Osprey Men-at-arms: The Soviet Army,* Albert Seaton
– *Uniforms illustrated 9: Soviet Army uniforms in World War two,* Steven J. Zaloga
– *Osprey Men-at-arms: The Red Army of the Great patriotic war,* Steven J. Zaloga
– *Ostfront - Hitler's war on Russia 1941-45,* Charles Winchester
– *Europa Militaria 14: Red Army uniforms of World War two,* Anton Shalito, Ilya Savchenkov and Andrew Mollo
– *Red Army uniforms 1918-45,* Anton Shalito, Ilya Savchenkov, Nikolay Roginsky and Kirill Tsyplenkov
– *articles in* Militaria Magazine, *by Gérard Gorokhoff (issues n°10, 21, 26, 32, 43, 53, 85, 105, 108, 128), P. Besnard (67 and 81), Robert Stedman (106 and 121), J. Rutkiewicz (195), and by the author (n° 192, 194, 206, 218, 220, 234, 236, 238, 261, 264, 266, 279, 281, 284, 306, 308 and 310).*
Back issues can be ordered at www.militaria-mag.com

Edited by Philippe Charbonnier, translated from the French by Lawrence Brown and Philippe Charbonnier
Design and layout by Philippe Charbonnier and Nathalie Sanchez, cover design by Gil Bourdeaux
© Histoire & Collections 2011

Published by
HISTOIRE & COLLECTIONS
5, avenue de la République F-75541 Paris Cedex 11
FRANCE

Tél. : 01 40 21 18 20
Fax 01 47 00 51 11
www.histoireetcollections.fr

This book has been designed, typed, laid-out and processed by Histoire & Collections and Le studio graphique A&C on fully integrated computer equipment

Printed by Zure, Spain EEC

July 2011